ANGELIC ENCOUNTERS

Over Fifty True Stories of Answered Prayer and Heavenly Intervention

Connalyn Allred

TEACH Services, Inc.
P U B L I S H I N G
www.TEACHServices.com • (800) 367-1844

World rights reserved. This book or any portion thereof may not be copied or reproduced in any form or manner whatever, except as provided by law, without the written permission of the publisher, except by a reviewer who may quote brief passages in a review.

The author assumes full responsibility for the accuracy of all facts and quotations as cited in this book. The opinions expressed in this book are the author's personal views and interpretations, and do not necessarily reflect those of the publisher.

This book is provided with the understanding that the publisher is not engaged in giving spiritual, legal, medical, or other professional advice. If authoritative advice is needed, the reader should seek the counsel of a competent professional.

Copyright © 2024 Connalyn Allred
Copyright © 2024 TEACH Services, Inc.
ISBN-13: 978-1-4796-1762-3 (Paperback)
ISBN-13: 978-1-4796-1763-0 (ePub)
Library of Congress Control Number: 2024916553

All scripture quotations are taken from the King James Version. Public domain.

Published by

DEDICATION

To my precious family. May we never forget the science of prayer or lose faith in our Father's willingness to answer prayer in times of need.

DEDICATION

TABLE OF CONTENTS

Introduction		vii
Chapter 1:	The God of Details	9
Chapter 2:	The God of Dreams	13
Chapter 3:	Some Angels Are Busier	21
Chapter 4:	Before They Call	24
Chapter 5:	A Brand from the Burning	27
Chapter 6:	A Caliper and a Compassionate Heart	30
Chapter 7:	The Battle Was Won	33
Chapter 8:	Fighting the Devil	38
Chapter 9:	A Child Unattended	43
Chapter 10:	Two Kinds of Mothers	47
Chapter 11:	God's Faithful Provisions	52
Chapter 12:	Trusting God's Timing	57
Chapter 13:	The Promise	62
Chapter 14:	Impossible Goals	65
Chapter 15:	The Interpreter	70
Chapter 16:	Even the Wind and Rain Obey Him	72
Chapter 17:	God's Generous Hand	75
Chapter 18:	Jesus Loves the Little Children	77
Chapter 19:	The Power of Prayer	83
Chapter 20:	Angels around Us	90

Chapter 21:	Helpers in Times of Need	95
Chapter 22:	Traveling on Air	100
Chapter 23:	Stranger in the Night	102
Chapter 24:	Sometimes Pretty, Sometimes Not	107
Chapter 25:	Angel Voices	112
Chapter 26:	The Precise Invasion	117
Chapter 27:	Steps to Answered Prayer	123
Bibliography		127

INTRODUCTION

Many times, we have experiences that can only be explained as divine interventions, celestial touchdowns, if you will. You may have encountered several in your own lifetime: the last-minute answers to your prayers; the near accidents that didn't happen; the strange circumstances that met your financial needs; the friend or stranger whose words carried you through an emotional crisis. We have all experienced major or minor miracles in our lives, but, as life becomes busier and busier, it is easy to disregard all of this as happenstance or chance. Sometimes, these touches with heaven are forgotten as we race through life.

The stories in this book are true, first-person accounts with the main points told to the author. Others are stories relayed by family members because the key participant is incapacitated or deceased. In some cases, name of people and places have been changed to ensure privacy, but dates and the main outline of these stories are reliable.

The process of interviewing various people for this book has proved to be an intriguing experience. As they talked, I typed as quickly as possible, trying to keep up with them. I copied sentences, phrases, and specific adjectives as they spoke. Their voices sometimes betrayed much emotion and even awe as they recalled their encounter with God's intervention in their lives. My attention was caught, as I sensed their deep feelings while they recounted these benchmark experiences. Many of the words spoken as they described their experiences could not be improved upon, and three friends gave me permission to copy their written rendition of their experiences, so, in that sense, this book has been written by those who were interviewed in addition to me as the author.

The interviewees' personal stories increased my faith in God and in His amazing love for each one of us. They also reminded me of the reality of God's presence in each of our lives, which can easily be forgotten as we actively pursue all that draws our attention in our everyday living.

> *If you have ever been tempted to believe our Father in heaven is not involved in your life, turn the page and read Roger's story.*

It is my prayer that these stories will inspire within you a deeper love for our Father in heaven and a determination to stay close to His leading as you make all your decisions each day. And…if you have ever been tempted to believe our Father in heaven is not involved in your life, turn the page and read Roger's story. No one can convince Roger that God doesn't know every detail of our existence.

CHAPTER 1

THE GOD OF DETAILS

Once again, Roger adjusted the baby carrier on his back as he took a long step on the path. He and baby Jonas had gone for a hike, and now Roger was headed home. It was nap time for baby Jonas, and Roger knew nap times were very important for the baby and for peace in the family.

Suddenly, Jonas began to cry and cry and cry. "What's the matter, Buddy?" Roger reached back to figure out what was causing all the commotion. Unable to find anything wrong, he slipped the carrier off his shoulders and checked the baby and everything in the carrier. Then it hit him! Jonas's pacifier was missing. "Oh, no," he groaned. The pacifier was everything to baby Jonas, and nap time would be impossible without it.

Quickly, Roger put the crying baby back in the carrier, mounted it on his shoulders, and retraced his steps. How does one find a small pacifier in a world of grass, weeds, and sticks? Looking everywhere on the trail, in the grass, and behind trees without success, Roger began to sense a mild panic entering his mind. He had to find that pacifier if Jonas's crying was going to stop!

Then it occurred to him. God knew where that pacifier was. Why not pray about this problem? "Dear God," he prayed. "You know how important that pacifier is to Jonas. Please show me where it is." Instantly, Roger saw a picture in his mind of a wooden box in the third barn on their property. "I wonder if God is trying to tell me something," he mused as he thought about the strong impression the picture had made on his thinking.

Once again, adjusting the baby carrier on his back as Jonas continued to cry, Roger headed towards the barn. Entering the barn, he saw many boxes piled up there, but in the middle was a wooden box he had seen in his mind a few minutes before. As he leaned over to look at its contents, on the top, you guessed it, was Jonas's pacifier! Quickly retrieving the pacifier, he handed it to the baby, and the crying stopped. Jonas was now content, and the Lord had answered yet another prayer, even a prayer to find a pacifier.

*****

Philippians 4:19 promises, "But my God shall supply all your need according to his riches in glory by Christ Jesus." Does this include physical, emotional, financial, and spiritual needs? Holly had the following stories to tell about how our Father in heaven supplied her needs. Our God is One who knows every detail of our lives, and Holly's stories illustrate how true this is. Here is her first story:

*****

Holly, who was fifteen at this time, experienced an incident that almost led to tragedy: she had been present when her brother was swimming and came close to drowning. No one else was available to save him, and Holly did the heroic act of saving his life. It was such a traumatic event for her that she almost gave up swimming altogether, but, after analyzing the whole picture, she decided to take swimming lessons twice a week and to complete a lifeguard training course. She had received certification papers that she kept in her wallet.

One day, while at the pool, she returned to the locker room and discovered that her wallet was missing from her locker. She had failed to lock the locker! Then began her search under benches, through lockers, on the top of the lockers, in the trash cans—and as she searched, she prayed, "Lord, I surrender this to you. I can't find my wallet, and my strength is at an end.

I need those certification papers. Please help me find my wallet! You've led me on this journey to be a lifeguard, and I'm asking for your help!"

Maybe I forgot it at home, she thought. But after thoroughly searching at home, the wallet was nowhere to be found. She called the school and asked for the janitorial staff to keep their eyes open for the missing wallet. For two days she searched and searched. Again, she found herself checking out the locker room. When she was about to head out the door, suddenly, Holly thought she saw a sock on top of the locker. Out of curiosity, she decided to look more closely, and there it was! The elusive wallet was sitting right where she had checked before. And best of all, only three pennies were missing.

She now had her lifeguard certification papers! With a sigh of relief and a smile on her face, Holly knew, once again, that God answers prayers for even the smallest details of our lives. Whether our Father in heaven impressed someone who had taken the wallet to return it or had arranged for it to be returned in another way, Holly didn't know. She was simply happy her prayers had been answered.

*****

We are told that when the heart of disbelief, a stony and rebellious heart, is transformed to a believing heart, a loving heart, a heart of flesh, it is the work of God's grace. We are also told how this grace is obtained.

"Go to your closet, and there alone plead with God: 'Create in me a clean heart, O God; and renew a right spirit within me.' Be in earnest, be sincere.... Jacoblike, wrestle in prayer. Agonize.... You must make an effort" (*Testimonies for the Church*, vol. 1, p. 158).

*****

Holly tells how faith-filled prayers changed her doubting heart to a happy, faith-filled heart, and it all happened while she was in high school. During those early years of secondary school, Holly struggled with horrible thoughts that she could never be saved. In fact, the struggle became so severe that she determined to simply leave God behind. After all, she concluded, if she was going to be lost regardless, why bother serving God now?

Fortunately, the Holy Spirit continued to reach Holly's heart, and by her senior year in academy, Holly decided to test God to see if He really was faithful.

> *Holly decided to test God to see if He really was faithful.*

She needed help with finances for tuition since she was basically responsible for her expenses at school. She worked hard at many jobs. It meant getting up early to make breakfast for the school five days a week. She worked overtime, but even fitting in extra hours of work, she still had less than half of what she needed to be debt-free at the end of the school year. It was a discouraging situation.

And so, Holly prayed. She had been taught the ABCs of prayer—Ask, Believe, and Claim the promises of God by thanking Him before the evidence is seen that He has answered the prayer. "Lord," she earnestly prayed, "I've worked hard, but I can't pay tithe [her work hours were directly applied to her bill]. You have said in Malachi 3:10 that if we bring the tithes into the storehouse then You will open the windows of heaven and pour us out a blessing so large that there won't be room enough to receive it. So, Lord, You are faithful. I believe You will help me with this school bill and help me pay tithe." After that prayer, Holly had peace of mind.

Two weeks later, Holly received a check for thirty-five dollars from the swimming pool department. She was tempted to put this on her school bill but decided to give it as a thank offering because she knew God was going to help her pay her school bill.

One evening, she noticed that a part of her amateur radio set was missing. She prayed for God to help her find the part. An impression was given her to remove the books on the bottom of the bookshelf in her room. She walked to the bookshelf, removed the books, and found what she was looking for. Praising God, she again said, "Thank you. Lord, for helping me find this. I know You'll take care of my school bill also."

She ran to her mother to tell her of her find when her mother said, "I haven't told you yet, but I've received word that an anonymous donor has committed to paying your school bill until the end of the year."

Holly's heart was now rejoicing in the knowledge that God is truly faithful in supplying our needs. Holly asked God, believed in His willingness to help her, and claimed His promise to do so. She found He truly loves those who put their faith in Him, and, with God, nothing is impossible.

CHAPTER 2

THE GOD OF DREAMS

Some people believe in dreams. Others put no credence in them at all. However, if a dream completely reverses the direction of one's life for the better, one can safely entertain the thought that it was divine intervention. Read Martin's story and see if you agree.

*****

Martin grew up in a Seventh-day Adventist pastor's home. Morning and evening worship was part of the daily schedule in the Sumerlin's home, and Martin learned to love Jesus and the Bible stories that he learned at home and in church school. At age ten he was baptized into the church, and his great desire was to be a preacher like his father. To encourage Martin's vision for his future, his father prepared mini-sermons for Martin to share in church.

Through an older relative, Martin and his brother, Dan, were eventually encouraged to eat meat, drink soda, go to the movies, smoke cigarettes, drink alcohol, play poker, and watch spiritually demoralizing television programs. All of this was against the Adventist lifestyle in which they had been raised. These boys raced faster and faster on the downward spiral.

This was the era of Elvis Presley, and the two boys did what they could to imitate him. Greasy duck-tail hairdos, leather jackets, jeans, and white suede shoes were the order of the day, and Martin and Dan followed suit. Soon, they joined the Road Runners Motorcycle Club. Martin was sixteen at the time. About half of the Road Runners were ex-Hell's Angels and, when the Road Runners folded, they went back to the Hell's Angels. It was then that Martin and his brother attended Hell's Angels parties, rode with them, used drugs, alcohol, cigarettes, and learned to swear prolifically.

Because of his devotion to our Father in heaven, Martin's dad decided to resign his position as the pastor of his church. He had read 1 Timothy 3:5, "(For if a man know not how to rule his own house, how shall he take care of the church of God?)" All in all, Martin's father had devoted fifty-three years of his life to pastoral work. During the many years that Martin and his brother were living a profligate life, their parents, grandparents, aunts, and uncles were praying tirelessly for them.

By seventeen years of age, Martin was married and became a father by age eighteen. He had not completed his schooling, so he had to work multiple low-paying jobs to support his family. All this time, he continued to play in a rock band. For sixteen years he turned his back on God, the church, and religion.

During this time, he was aware that God was trying to gain his attention. He was in a terrible car accident that claimed the life of his unborn child. After this, he became wilder and immersed himself in burglaries and drugs until he was arrested and sentenced to four years in the juvenile prison. Through his father's invention, the judge agreed instead to sentence Martin to four years of probation. After two and a half years, his probation officer told him he would dissolve the charges if Martin "kept his nose clean." Martin stayed out of trouble, and his record was expunged.

After he and his wife divorced, he continued to play in the band and take methamphetamines—to the point that he overdosed in 1968. This experience could have killed him, but a divine hand overruled, and Martin continued to live. He suffered migraine headaches for two months after the overdose.

When he was thirty years of age, Martin's mother took drastic action. She began claiming the promise found in Isaiah 57:21, "There is no peace, saith my God, to the wicked." Never underestimate a godly mother's prayers! They are powerful, and our Father in heaven was very sensitive to listening to the cries of Martin's mother.

Suddenly, everything seemed to go wrong in Martin's life. In the past, he had always been able to put a band together in two weeks to play in a nightclub, but now he could not get any two guys to agree on songs they were going to play, who was going to sing it, and who was going to play the lead, etc. Furthermore, there was trouble at home between Martin and his girlfriend. Worse yet, his three children made it clear that they wanted to live the same kind of life he was living. This truly scared him! Also, the people he was buying drugs from as well as some of those who he was selling drugs to were arrested. Martin realized he would probably be the next to be arrested.

And then, something happened that changed his life. It was a complete 180-degree turn, in fact. This is how it happened. Martin will tell it in his own words:

> I had the most vivid dream I have ever had in my life! I dreamed I was walking out into a field and saw an open well, the kind with a ladder inside. I thought it was the opportunity to find a pirate's treasure: gold, silver, jewels, and other valuables. I began my descent, and after going down about five rungs on the ladder, I noticed the sun had crossed over the well, and it even seemed like it was getting darker! I thought, *I don't have a flashlight or rope, and no one knows I am out here.*
>
> I started back up, and the rung I was standing on and the one in my hands broke, and I fell to the bottom of the well! Guess what! No treasures—only mud and a little water. I was in the pit, and I looked up and tried to scale the walls that were about four feet apart. They were slippery, and I just slid to the bottom. I looked up, and it was apparent that the only way I would ever get out of there was for someone to pull me out.
>
> I immediately awakened and knew it was God trying to tell me something! I recognized that each rung of the ladder that I descended was disobedience to parents, drinking soda, smoking cigarettes, drinking alcohol, swearing, lying, stealing, and violating all of the Ten Commandments! I was just staring and thinking about this new revelation!

My partner, Monica, awakened and said, "What is going on? It's only 5 o'clock! You don't get up for another hour and a half."

I related the dream to her and said, "We are quitting drugs and alcohol today!"

Unimpressed, she scoffed, "Oh yeah, we have been through this before! I quit for two days, and you quit for two hours, and then we both were back using as usual."

"That is because we have been making promises to God, to each other, our families, and friends or anyone that will still listen, and we do not have the power to do it!" I exclaimed. "We need to pray to God and claim His promises!" I had learned this solution so many years ago, while attending Wal-Mar Junior Academy, now named Pleasant Hill Adventist Academy.

Monica responded, "You will have to pray. I don't know how."

I claimed a promise that I had never memorized, Ezekiel 36:26, 27. I was amazed, but God brought it back to my memory because I had read the whole Bible three times before I turned into a prodigal son!

I prayed, "God, You promised in Ezekiel 36:26, 27, 'A new heart also will I give you, and a new spirit will I put within you: and I will take away the stony heart out of your flesh, and I will give you an heart of flesh. And I will put my spirit within you, and cause you to walk in my statues, and ye shall keep my judgments, and do them.'"

I also claimed Philippians 4:13, "I can do all things through Christ which strengtheneth me." I said, "God, you know we have tried many times and always fail miserably. Please take away the taste and desire for all things that are out of harmony with You." That was August 4, 1977. God is faithful! I celebrated His faithfulness this month of forty-four years since He took it all away!

Now began a new life for Martin and Monica. They moved far away from the drug friends and closer to their spiritually-minded family. They were married January 1, 1978, and they were baptized together on February 18 that same year.

While talking with one of his uncles, who was a physician, Martin complained that he had almost no short-term memory. His uncle explained that Martin had destroyed millions of brain cells with the use of drugs, cigarettes, and alcohol. However, there was hope. His uncle explained that God could heal his brain and then gave him three steps to follow:

1. Ask God to send the Holy Spirit to guide you into all truth as Jesus promised in John 16:13.
2. Study God's Word daily.
3. Share what you learn!

Martin has followed this advice for forty-four years! He has shared his story in churches, schools, two prisons, Bible study groups, one-on-one, and any time he knows that someone is struggling with an addiction. It is the good news for Martin and for those who will listen to him. He has also been on the radio for nine years preaching, sharing topical Bible studies, interviewing pastors, doctors and other health professionals, attorneys, a scientist, former lesbians, and other Christians who share their testimonies. Martin firmly believes that anyone, regardless of their sins and failures, can be healed by God if they come to Him in faith! Martin is currently the head elder in his local church and has been loving that position for twenty years.

In closing, Martin has this to say, "My advice to parents and young people regarding spiritual growth, what to avoid, staying close to the Lord, etc. is to involve them in ministry. Do not try to just entertain them with music and being their buddy while excusing poor choices. My mother's solution was, 'We will do what is right because it is right!' Do just what my Uncle Charles advised me to do. Ask for the Holy Spirit to guide you, study the Bible every day, and share what you have learned with others. God will bless you, too!"

Once again, honest-hearted parents experienced wonderful answers to their prayers. They continued praying in faith even though the answers were many years in coming. Praise God for faithful, praying, Christian parents! Praise God He will save us from our sins!

*****

The Babylonian monarch, Nebuchadnezzar, was impressed by a God-sent dream so many years ago. Our Father in heaven doesn't limit this kind of communication to monarchs, however. Elena's story tells us heaven-sent dreams are one of the ways God still uses to gives us direction.

*****

The year was 1961. The place was communist Romania. Elena, a young mother, had been attending the Seventh-day Adventist Church and had realized this church used the Bible as the basis for its doctrines. As she listened to the sermons, a conviction grew in her heart that she must join this church, but steps had to be taken with the government to get permission before she could join. So, Elena approached the head elder.

"I would like to be baptized," she explained. "Would you fill out the necessary paperwork, so I can have permission to join this church?"

The elder looked at her quizzically. "Are you sure you want to join this church? You know that you will have many hardships if you join this church. I think you had better think about that. I don't recommend that you join this church!"

Taken aback, Elena thought, *This doesn't sound right.*

During that era of complete communist control, informants who appeared to be sincere church members had been placed in the churches as spies. Not knowing this, Elena was confused by the elder's response.

Elena's deep desire to be baptized had been crushed, and she went home crying. Her husband, Florin, sensed immediately that she needed encouragement. Although Florin was not a church member, he had been a good husband to Elena, so he was concerned.

"The head elder told me not to be baptized," Elena sobbed out her heartbreak.

"Do you believe what you have learned?" Florin's voice was somber.

"Yes."

"Do you believe it is the truth?"

"Yes."

"Do you believe God is leading you to do this?"

"Yes."

"Then," his face had a look of earnestness, "don't look to the right or to the left. You must be baptized."

Elena paused. "But I just don't know."

"Have you prayed about it?"

"Yes."

Still in a state of uncertainty, Elena prayed again.

Shortly after that, she had a dream. In her dream she was walking down a long hallway which had several doors on one side. As she walked, she had a sense of urgency. Which door should she enter? Door number one? No, that was not the one. Door number two? No. Number three? Again, the answer was no. And on and on until she came to door number seven. A being dressed in white stepped out and motioned to the open door.

With a gentle, commanding tone he said, "This is the way, walk ye in it." Elena had her answer.

With confidence she approached the head elder once again. "I've decided to be baptized. Please arrange for the government papers to be sent in for permission. I want to join this church." The permission was granted, and Elena was joyfully baptized. She was a young woman who was willing to go through any hardship for Christ's sake, and God had sent the dream to lead her to her final decision.

*****

The biblical story of the prophet Elisha and the bears teaches that God's servants should be respected and honored. Elisha had just witnessed Elijah's departure from this world in a fiery chariot and was on his way to Bethel when a group of young people met him. Here's what happened next:

> And he [Elisha] went from thence unto Bethel: and as he was going up by the way, there came forth little children out of the city, and mocked him, and said unto him, Go up, thou bald head; go up, thou bald head. And he turned back, and looked on them, and cursed them in the name of the LORD. And there came forth two she bears out of the wood, and tare forty and two children of them. (2 Kings 2:23, 24)

This experience sobered the entire nation of Israel so that Elisha, as a prophet of God, was never ridiculed or made fun of again. The following story shows how the story of Elisha and the bears is still making its impact today—and our Father in heaven used a dream to do it.

*****

The bears raced from the woods intent on destroying the young men. Screams and yells split the air as the youth fled…but let's start at the beginning to see how this story began.

Ron was a young man who faithfully attended church and had many friends there. One group of friends were highly educated; they were so much fun and very witty. Ron, having an out-going personality, fit right in and was even the life of the party, at times.

As he and his friends met together, some would talk occasionally about the pastor's poor grammar. The group would make fun of the poor speech they had heard in the last sermon. The pastor became a topic of conversation and many a good laugh.

At times, Ron would join in the mocking fun and felt justified in correcting the pastor's English errors. Until, one night, Ron had a dream. In this dream, he saw Elisha and the young men who were mocking God's servant. "Go up, thou bald head. Go up." Instantly, she-bears emerged from the forest and attacked the young men, seriously mauling them.

Ron awakened from his dream. His attention was fully aroused, and he instantly knew why he had been sent this dream. "Oh my," he lamented," I've been defacing one of God's servants." He was deeply convicted that what he had done was very wrong. That day, he called the pastor and told him he would like to take him to lunch.

As they ate lunch together, Ron confessed he had not supported the pastor and had joined with others in not supporting him. Ron explained what the issues were—the pastor's sermons. Ron made a suggestion. He felt it would be helpful if the pastor tape recorded his sermons and listened carefully to how they were delivered. Also, Ron promised, "As long as I am here, I will do what I can to give you 100 percent support." The pastor, realizing Ron's sincerity and the apparent need to improve his sermons, thanked Ron and took his suggestions about reviewing his sermons before he preached. He did just that, and, for the benefit of all, his delivery style improved.

So, once again, our Father in heaven intervened to turn a negative pattern of several people's interaction and a pastor's weakness into something positive for His faithful servant, and He did it through a dream!

CHAPTER 3

SOME ANGELS ARE BUSIER

As we analyze various professions, trades, and occupations, we recognize that there is much greater risk in some than in others. Such is the case for loggers. These men must always be aware of the "widow makers:" the large trees or limbs that unexpectedly fall a different direction.

Stan is a man of prayer, and he had four stories to share in which he could easily have been killed. However, God had another plan for Stan. His first story illustrates the dangers loggers face daily.

*****

"We had a landing above where we were logging where we could load the logs on the truck. The trucker up above us decided he didn't want one of the logs, so he pushed it over the edge. That log hit me in the head, and, fortunately, the hard hat I was wearing lessened the blow. Without it, I most certainly would have been killed. The impact of the log sent me down over the hill, and I spent three days in the hospital. While there, I couldn't move without seeing stars. Our pastor came to visit me, and it was about a half hour before I recognized it was my pastor.

When they were ready to discharge me from the hospital, they asked if I hurt any place else. I told them there was a tingling in my wrist, so an x-ray was taken. The x-ray showed a compound fracture, and I was in a cast for six months."

*****

Stan tells of another logging experience when he was trying to put a choker on a log. It was a large log about three feet in diameter, and he couldn't find a good spot to place the choker. He walked the log, crawled under it on the downhill side, and walked the uphill side to locate the right place for the choker. Because his shoelace was untied, he put his foot on the log to tie his shoe. He was on the uphill side of the log. That small amount of pressure caused the huge log to roll over the edge and downhill. With sudden realization, Stan had the chilling thought that the log could have rolled when he was under it on the downhill side. Saved once more!

*****

> *Suddenly, the engine died and he began to roll quickly downhill.*

Another time, Stan was clearing brush for a logging road that was to have a 15 percent grade. However, the areas he needed to clear were steeper than 15 percent. On one of the steep slopes, Stan tried to remove a large stump. Suddenly, the engine died on the old machine he was driving, and he began to roll quickly downhill. Pumping the brakes, he found they were not working, so Stan knew he must jump from the machine. That jump was seven or eight feet to the ground, and he landed on one foot. The impact shattered his ankle, but his decision to jump saved his life. The machine traveled several hundred feet and finally hit a large tree. The impact would surely have killed Stan, but he was saved one more time.

*****

The last story Stan had to a share involved his project of building a pole barn. Before building the barn, he had decided to cut down a tree near the building site. For reasons he didn't understand at the time, he was impressed to cut the stump off level with the ground. What a blessing that proved to be!

Later, as he was putting the ridge rafters up, Stan fell off the ladder and landed on his back in exactly the same spot where the tree had stood. If the stump had been there, the injury would have been much worse, but he did not break his back, and he was in the hospital for only two days.

*****

A statement from the book *Evangelism* seems to explain who guided Stan to cut the stump down. "To all who will walk humbly with God He will give His Holy Spirit and will minister to them through the agency of holy angels to make right impressions upon human minds" (*Evangelism*, p. 629). Stan knows that someday, in God's heavenly kingdom, his guardian angel will explain all the times he saved Stan from certain death. These four stories may be only the tip of the iceberg. Thank God for heavenly protection and for angels who guide us through strong impressions!

CHAPTER 4

BEFORE THEY CALL

Have you ever been caught in a situation where you didn't have time to call on God for help? Isaiah 65:24 tells us God's promise: "…Before they call, I will answer; and while they are yet speaking, I will hear." There are reasons we are encouraged to lay our plans at the feet of Jesus every morning and to ask for His protection throughout the day. Thirteen people from a Christian church in Central Point, Oregon, didn't have time to call out for divine intervention, but they learned the value of morning worship. Read their story and understand why.

*****

"Yeah! We get to go rafting!"

After a week of hard work building Project Patch's administration building in Idaho, a group of Christian volunteers from Oregon were looking forward to the fun of floating down the Payette River. Some of the young people had floated down that river the day before and had had a great time with no problems, so the group of thirteen people, which included a six-year-old boy, jumped into cars and a van to begin their happy excursion.

As they approached the river and looked down, the rapids appeared to be quite steep, but, remembering how the young folks had conquered the river the day before, they began loading in a navy survival raft. It needs to be noted here that these rafts are made for the ocean, not for rivers with steep rapids. Unknown to the rafters was that a lot of snow on the mountains had melted during the previous twenty-four hours, and the river was about two feet higher now with class three rapids. A dangerous situation indeed!

Harold stood at the front of the raft holding on to ropes threaded through poles. The rocky ride soon brought the raft to a fork in the river, and right there at the fork was a huge boulder. *We're going to hit that boulder!* Harold thought as they sped towards the fork. *We're going to be thrown off this raft!* And that is exactly what happened!

In seconds, Harold found himself under the raft with a rope tied around his foot which he could not untangle even with effort. Again, he thought, *Kick it free.* Giving it a mighty kick, he was able to free himself from the rope but was soon being bounced along the rapids.

By this time, the camp director and the pastor had been able to climb onto the bottom of the over-turned raft and, with their help, Harold also crawled on the raft. Fortunately, two kayakers were positioned on the side of the river, and one of them threw a rope to Harold, but the violence of the river pulled the rope from his hand. A second rope was thrown. This time Harold wrapped it around his hand, and it held.

Now that they were pulled to shore, the three men began to search for the other ten rafters. Everyone was able to make it to shore. Even though there were minor injuries, all ten of the remaining rafters survived. This was miraculous considering the level of the rapids and the danger that confronted them in a matter of seconds.

A sheriff surveying the river and what had just happened stated, "You guys are crazy!" Considering the level of the rapids and the type of raft they were using, the group was humbled when realizing what could have happened. They now knew huge rapids should never be part of a river rafting excursion, and, yes, the type of raft used is very important. Lessons were learned the hard way that day.

That evening, during vespers time, many thanks ascended to heaven for protection from what could have been multiple tragedies. All the dramatic events of the day had happened so quickly that there was no time to pray. Before they could call, God had answered. They now remembered they had asked for God's protection that morning during worship time. He had not failed them.

CHAPTER 5

A BRAND FROM THE BURNING

The story of Shadrach, Meshach, and Abednego's deliverance from the burning, fiery furnace may appear to be almost unbelievable to some. It is certainly believable to Bruce. His experience in the deadliest and most destructive fire in California's history proved to him that our Father in heaven is all-powerful, and He can save even in the most dangerous situations. Bruce's story will increase your faith in God's ability to protect in all circumstances if He chooses to do so.

*****

With fire on both sides, Bruce hit the gas pedal and traveled through the smoke barely able to see. The occupants in his car were frightened, and all were praying. How had they gotten into this situation?

Six years before, in 2012, Bruce and Millie Brown had moved to Paradise, California, after he had accepted a position as a chaplain for

Hillside Hospital. Three weeks after their move to Paradise, Millie was diagnosed with stage four colon cancer, and the struggle for survival now began. Initially, the family felt Millie would win this battle. But, as time wore on, Millie realized that she would not be okay, so her focus was to make sure her children would be prepared for life. Music lessons, homeschool, as many fun excursions as she could endure became the rhythm of their lives. When Ali, the youngest child, graduated from the eighth grade, she was given a five-hundred-dollar scholarship awarded to students who demonstrated spiritual maturity and scholastic excellence. After Bruce told Millie of Ali's prize, he feels she concluded that her children were going to be alright. Millie passed away one week later.

November 8, 2018, began as any other day, with Bruce encouraging his two children to leave for school while he prepared to go to work. Once his children arrived at school, however, they were told to return home. The worst fire in the history of California was now surrounding the city of Paradise, and evacuation plans were escalating. When Bruce arrived at the hospital, he immediately knew everyone needed to move quickly to evacuate patients.

The fire, which sounded like a train, could be heard coming up the canyon. Calling his sixteen-year-old son, who had earned his driver's license a mere three weeks before, Bruce said, "Hook the trailer to the pick-up, load your sister, your grandmother, our pets, and our valuable documents in the trailer as quickly as possible. Paradise is surrounded by fire, so leave very quickly." Justin, his son, had not hooked the trailer to the pick-up nor had driven the pick-up before, but he did as he was told.

Back at the hospital, ambulances were called for the patients until no more ambulances were available. Then nurses, doctors, and other staff began transporting patients. Bruce was the last to leave the hospital grounds. His van was the transport for two ICU patients and one mute hospice patient who were very frightened when realizing their danger.

Once on the road, travel was very slow because hundreds were trying to escape the inferno. Fire now was on both sides of their car, and, in an effort to calm his patients, Bruce said, "Let's pray!" And pray they did! Remembering the biblical story of the three Hebrews who had escaped Nebuchadnezzar's fiery furnace, Bruce prayed, "Lord, please protect us as You did Shadrach, Meshach, and Abednego from the burning, fiery furnace!" Realizing the strong possibility of his car going up in flames, Bruce called his son. "I love you. I want to say goodbye because I may not make it out. Tell your sister I love her, too!"

Eventually, Bruce spotted a sheriff and asked him to help them get out, for he needed to get these patients to a hospital. The sheriff left and returned to tell Bruce that he could not find a way out. Later, after more searching, the sheriff led Bruce and his patients to an exit. Then Bruce, who could not see ahead because of the smoke, took the risk of racing down the road, not knowing what he might encounter.

Finally, around 3:00 p.m., Bruce was able to reach a hospital with his patients. To everyone's relief, the patients were quickly taken in. Later, Bruce learned all the patients from his hospital had been successfully evacuated.

Now he took time to see if his children and their grandmother had escaped the fire. Yes, they had made it to safety, and he learned their location. Their reunion was an unforgettable moment. Bruce said he had never hugged his children so tightly in such a long embrace. Many prayers of thanks ascended to our Father in heaven, and many tears of gratefulness were shed.

But what about his home? Had it survived? Eventually, Bruce was allowed to go down his driveway, and there it stood. The guest house had burned, his neighbor's home had burned, but his home was still in one piece. Friends and family had prayed very specifically that his home would not be destroyed, knowing all the loss Bruce and his children had already endured with Millie's death. Those prayers were also honored by heaven.

What is to be learned from this unforgettable ordeal? A few of the lessons learned could be that our Father in heaven gives wisdom and expertise when we are under stress (such as an inexperienced teenager transporting his family to safety); He can provide peace and calmness in the most trying circumstances; and, if He wills it, He can provide safety even in the middle of an inferno. Prayer was an integral part of Bruce and his family's experience before and during the Paradise fire. Prayer is still the bedrock of their everyday lives. Thank God for His many answers to the prayers of His people!

CHAPTER 6

A CALIPER AND A COMPASSIONATE HEART

Sometimes answers to our prayers come in a rough-looking package. Such was the case when Holly's brakes were needing repair. Holly was nervous about the man's exterior, but she found he had a big, compassionate heart.

*****

Woosh! It sounded like a jet flying over. *What is going on here?* Holly thought. She was traveling from southern Seattle to Mt. Lassen, and her car kept making this *wooshing* sound. As a young, twenty-four-year-old woman, she was cautious about traveling alone on Interstate 5—and now this. Since she was about four hours away from home and didn't know anyone in this area, she stopped at a Costco to get gas and to see if she could locate the problem. Walking around her car, she noticed the brake caliper on the right front tire had worn down until it had burned the brake pad. What to do?

Calling her friend who had worked on her car's brakes several weeks before, Holly explained her situation. It was Sunday, mechanics were off duty, and she knew no one in the area. "Call around to the automotive parts stores and find the best deal on a caliper," he suggested. "Ask if they know of a mechanic who can help you." Finally, she found the best price and purchased the caliper.

Off and on, throughout the day, Holly had been praying. "Dear God. I need your help. I believe You will help me get the car fixed. Thank You in advance for helping me."

Another friend texted that she should go into Costco's tire center and get directions from their crew. Holly began to pray again, asking for wisdom, guidance, and a divine appointment, if it was God's will. Again, she thanked God for His help.

As she entered Costco, she saw a group of elderly people entering at the same time and she began to question many of them: "Do you live in the area? Do you know of a mechanic who works on Sunday?" The answers were always in the negative.

Once again, standing in line at the Costco tire center, Holly patiently waited for her turn when she heard an older man ask, "What's that on the back of your t-shirt? I've been trying to read it." There was a Bible text on the back of her shirt, and so the conversation started.

"Do you live locally?" Holly reiterated her question. "Can you recommend a mechanic who could help me today?"

"What do you need done?"

"I need a caliper replaced. I have the part, but I don't have the tools to do it myself."

"Well, if you have the part, I have the tools. If you come to my place, I'll fix it for you."

Here was a total stranger offering to fix her car, if she would come to his place. Holly's reticence was understandable, but the car really needed fixing, so she called her friend who was a former police officer to ask his advice. "Go ahead and go to his place. Just give me the address and stay on the phone with me. If there's any trouble, I'll call the authorities to help you out."

With that assurance, Holly drove to the address she'd been given. The older man's girlfriend chatted incessantly while her boyfriend fixed the caliper. All in all, after being given a tour of their place, the whole experience took two hours.

Thanking her benefactor profusely, Holly once again began her journey south. She determined to later send a thank you note and a copy of *The Desire of Ages* to the kind older man, who was the answer to her prayers. And now her prayers to our Father in heaven were full of praise for a seemingly impossible situation had been solved through the help of a total stranger.

Holly's experience reminds us of a quotation found in the book, *Christ's Object Lessons*:

> God does not say, Ask once, and you shall receive. He bids us ask. Unweariedly persist in prayer. The persistent asking brings the petitioner into a more earnest attitude, and gives him an increased desire to receive the things for which he asks. Christ said to Martha at the grave of Lazarus, "If thou wouldest believe, thou shouldest see the glory of God." (p. 145)

Holly's persistent prayers, her belief that God would find a solution to her problem, and thanking Him in advance for His help showed her faith. God honored her faith; the problem was solved; and she was able to safely continue her journey south.

CHAPTER 7

THE BATTLE WAS WON

Many Christian parents have prayed and prayed for years for their wayward son or daughter. Often, it seems the prayers are unanswered or, at least, put on the back burner of heaven while other prayers are obviously answered immediately. If you are one of those parents who have agonized over your children's choices and are fearful they will be lost, you will find the next story to be heart-warming. Yes, it took time for this young man to respond to the Holy Spirit's promptings, but, at last, the turnaround was made, and his wayward feet are, once again, firmly planted on the road towards heaven.

"We must pray as we never have before that God will keep and bless our children" (*Child Guidance*, p. 494). Keep praying, dear parents. Keep praying! Mike's story will encourage you.

*****

Michael Harrington was a likeable young man who had the privilege of being a third-generation Seventh-day Adventist and who had the privilege of growing up in a wonderful Adventist home. His parents were prayer warriors who believed in making sure their children had a solid Christian education, so Mike was sent to Adventist schools until he graduated from high school.

It was then that Mike began to hang out with the wrong crowd. It all probably started innocently at first, but soon his buddies were staying up late, smoking, doing drugs, etc. Methamphetamine became Mike's favorite drug because it wasn't as expensive as some of the other drugs. It gave a feeling of euphoria for three or four days, and he remembers when he went for seven days without sleep due to the "high" from meth.

All this time, Mike worked for a lumber company and never had a sick day. From all outward appearances, he was functioning normally until all the employees were required to be tested for drugs. Then his secret was found out, and he had to enter a drug treatment program, which was somewhat of a wakeup call for Mike. Regardless, he still smoked two packs of cigarettes a day.

All this time, his parents were faithfully praying, asking for deliverance from sin for their son. Nowadays, Mike so much appreciates his parents' prayers, and he believes his mother's prayers were especially heard by heaven. One of the many reasons he believes this can be illustrated by an experience he had at about 3:00 a.m. many years ago.

Mike and his friends had packaged drugs for Mike to sell, and he had stowed them behind the front seat of the car. After some heavy drinking, Mike and his wife began the trip home. They were stopped by the police, and Mike failed to walk the line. In fact, he was so drunk that he couldn't even remember his own address. Yes, he was drunk-drunk.

The police did not take him to jail, but they told Mike's wife to drive the car home. Mike now realizes if the police had discovered all those drugs behind the seat of the car, he would have probably been put in prison. Yes, his mother's prayers put a huge protection around him for many years!

Renae, the very same wife he was driving with that drunken night, was later killed in a traffic accident late at night. This was another wakeup call for Mike. If Mike heard a Christian song on the radio, he would get misty-eyed. News reports about bombings in the Middle East made him think, *I'd better get my life together. It's the end of the world!* Many times, the Holy Spirit impressed Mike's thinking, and the step-by-step process in returning to God was quietly taking place.

After twenty-six years of living a secular life that drove Mike to essentially homelessness, he found himself living with his dad. During those years, his praying mother had passed away without seeing her son return to the Lord. One day his dad announced, "Mike, Kenneth Cox is holding evangelistic meetings at the church. You ought to go with me. And did you know that Darren Smith is now an elder in the church?"

Darren Smith an elder in the church? Mike's mind reeled. Darren was an old drinking buddy of his, and he couldn't imagine Darren having changed that much. In the end, Mike decided to go to the meetings but, trying to be invisible, he sat way at the back of the church. Finally, Elder Cox made an appeal. "Those of you who would like to truly give your heart to Jesus, please just come up here to the front. I will pray with you."

Now the battle really began. The Holy Spirit impressed Mike to stand and go forward, but the devil was determined he would not do such a thing. Back and forth, Mike's mind raced as he fought the battle between good and evil. Finally, he stood and walked to the end of the pew and down the aisle, where he waited for the prayer to begin.

> *Back and forth, Mike's mind raced as he fought the battle.*

Now was a new life for Mike. His love for music led him to join the Oregon Men's Chorus, and he has traveled the world singing with this group for twenty-five years. Eventually, the Lord led him to meet a lovely Christian lady, and their marriage has been a blessing to many others as they have served in the local church. And, yes, Mike is now an elder in the church, and his wife teaches one of the adult Sabbath School classes.

Mike is so grateful that his life had been preserved while he lived recklessly. He is so grateful his voice has been preserved after smoking two packs a day. He is so grateful God is patient and long-suffering "not willing that any should perish" (2 Peter 3:9). What a great and loving God we serve!

*****

Sometimes, only grandparents know the Lord. Sometimes they are the only ones willing to pray for their grandchildren. Karen's story helps all of us realize the power of grandparents' prayers.

*****

The wind whipped past Karen's face as she sped the motorbike faster and faster down the freeway. With five-year-old Stan's back seat belted to her body, she knew she must drive carefully, but, oh, how she wanted to get away from this man she lived with. The faster, the better. Now three months pregnant, Karen was determined to keep her baby, but the father of this child insisted on an abortion. This made the decision easy for Karen. She would travel to her Aunt Jolene's home in Seattle, Washington, and leave this man behind. The long and risky trip took three days, and it even included staying awake all night in a rest stop, guarding her bike and shooing the cockroaches off Stan while he slept.

Life had not been easy for Karen. Her mother had left the family of three children and traveled west to California when Karen was very young. After that, Karen remembers traveling west as her dad brought Karen, her brother, and her sister there in an effort to reunite the family. In this new environment, the children were left with a drug-addicted babysitter, who would lock them outside to stay in the backyard.

Fortunately, with the children's protection in mind, her grandparents sold their home in the east, and for one year, the three young children lived with their grandparents. *Yes*, Karen thought, as she adjusted to life with Aunt Jolene, *Grandpa is the best man I have ever known*. He was a true Christian. Grandpa was not loud, but he was jovial. He was always happy, and his happiness was such a contrast to Karen's feelings, as she tried to build a new life for herself and her children.

Karen remembered that after arriving in California, her grandpa began the colporteur work, selling religious books door-to-door. Out of that meager income, he managed to send Karen and her older sister, Gladys, and younger brother, Keith, to the local Adventist school. He said many, many prayers for his three precious grandchildren because he understood how life had been very unfair to them already.

The years passed. Karen and her siblings grew up, and her grandpa died at age eighty-three. Gladys kept going to church, but Keith and Karen lived a profligate life filled with drugs, alcohol, children out of wedlock, and Keith even found himself in prison. It seemed that most of her grandpa's prayers and hard-earned money to send his grandchildren to the Adventist elementary school had been wasted.

One day, Karen met with Keith. He seemed different. He had a peace about him, and, amazingly, he had the same kind of happiness that she remembered her grandpa having. What was going on? Karen realized that Keith was going to church on Sabbath and attending prayer meetings on

Tuesday nights. Could this be the reason for Keith's new attitude? As Karen interacted with Keith, she was drawn to the truths she had learned as a young child. Soon she began attending church, then was hired as a teacher's aide in the local Adventist school. Her spiritual life continued to grow as she interacted with Christian friends and continually studied her Bible.

Today, Karen is a devout Christian who prays earnestly for her family and friends. Although, for many years it appeared that Karen and Keith's lives were out of focus with God, her grandpa's prayers prevailed in the end. What a happy reunion that will be when God's people enter the New Jerusalem, and Grandpa sees Gladys, Karen, and Keith among that throng! Eternal happiness, eternal joy, eternal gratefulness will be their theme song, and a grandfather's faithful prayers are very much a part of this happy ending.

CHAPTER 8

FIGHTING THE DEVIL

As we analyze the incredible temptations that face the youth of today, we realize the evil one attempts to derail even young children. However, be encouraged when you read Carly's story. Know that our Father in heaven will go to any extent to save our children.

*****

Beautiful strains of music floated over the small school room as the video of Fairhaven Academy's choir and orchestra was being shown during art class. Carly and her friend Cassie, both fourth graders, were very impressed with the video.

"I want to go there some day," Cassie whispered to Carly.

"Me too!" Carly's voice was emphatic.

"Let's write a letter to Fairhaven and tell them we want to be accepted there when we're in high school."

"Good idea!"

And so, two young fourth graders composed a letter to the school announcing their definite intentions to attend Fairhaven someday.

The years rolled by, and both girls eventually graduated from the eighth grade. Fairhaven did not accept freshmen, so Cassie and Carly attended two different high schools their freshman year. Cassie ultimately stayed in that same high school for four years.

However, life was different for Carly. She found that she did not fit in at her school her freshman year. At least, it started out that way. The other students had formed cliques; she didn't wear stylish clothes; she was socially awkward; and she was made fun of because she was adopted. Even a substitute teacher was difficult to deal with, and another freshman girl competed fiercely with Carly and became her worst enemy. Carly was miserable! Not only was she miserable at school but her attitude also carried over into her relationships at home. Soon, she found she was arguing with her mother every day.

As the weeks wore on, one of the most popular guys in the school began to talk with Carly. She complained to him how the others were treating her. Not long after, other students were apologizing to Carly. Her former enemy told her she genuinely felt badly about how she had been mean to Carly, and even the principal talked with the students about how unacceptable bullying was. All this time, Carly's mother and grandparents were praying that God would intervene for her.

Life began to look good. Carly now made many friends at the school, and she made up her mind that she would continue there her sophomore year. After all, she had a boyfriend, lots of girls were nice to her, her grades were excellent, and she had nothing to complain about.

Then Fairhaven called. This was the school that had a two-year waiting list and Carly had been on their list for only a year. "We've accepted you as a student for this next year, and we look forward to seeing you! We'll send you more information by email," the recording on the answering machine said. But now Carly did not want to go to Fairhaven Academy. She was perfectly happy with the school she was attending.

Mom exclaimed, "It's great Fairhaven has accepted you!"

"But I don't want to go there!" Carly started crying.

"I know that God wants you to go to Fairhaven," her mother replied. "I've been praying about it."

"No, mom. Unless God literally tells me that's where He wants me to go, I won't go." Carly was determined.

Carly's mother kept praying, and Carly kept praying, but they were opposite prayers.

"Dear God, please tell Carly she needs to go to Fairhaven." Mom's voice was pleading.

"Dear God, please convince my mother I shouldn't go to Fairhaven." Carly's voice was desperate.

That night, Carly's mother was at work, and Carly was home. A caregiver for her grandfather was also in the house. This evening while she was brushing her hair in the bathroom, Carly prayed a different prayer. "Dear God, if I'm supposed to go to Fairhaven, please convince me as much as my mother is convinced."

Suddenly, she heard her name called. "Carly!" Thinking the caregiver had called her, Carly went to the kitchen.

"Did you call me?"

"No, I didn't call you."

Going back to the bathroom, Carly heard her name being called again. The second time, she went to the kitchen.

"Did you call me?"

"No, dear, I didn't call you."

Back in the bathroom, Carly thought of Samuel and Eli. She prayed, "God, if this is You calling me, please speak to me one more time." She then heard the voice literally behind her. Below, Carly tells what happened.

> I fell on my knees because I couldn't stand any more. I can't explain it, but I felt transported as if I weren't in the bathroom anymore. Then God spoke in a clear, distinct voice, and said, "Carly, I know the school you're now in has been horrible to you. Even if Fairhaven is as bad, I will be with you." I answered, "What do You want me to do? No matter what it is, I'll do it."
>
> God answered me. "I want you to go to Fairhaven. That is where My plan is leading you." As soon as I said, "Okay," I felt I was back in the bathroom. I got up off my knees and began to cry. I was in awe of what happened to me.
>
> When my mother came home, she was very surprised when I told her I was going to Fairhaven. We both knew that God was directing me to Fairhaven Academy. It was so clear to us.

What a wonderful God we serve who is willing to answer prayers as He leads His children along! He is even willing to verbally direct a teenage girl to a school she didn't want to attend. The second part of Carly's story explains more details of God's intervention in her life and why He wanted her to attend Fairhaven Academy.

*****

Carly arrived at Fairhaven Academy excited to be where she knew she was supposed to be. The atmosphere was wonderful, and teachers and students were supportive of each other. The devil didn't like this kind of spiritual progress, so he began to tempt Carly to do little, very little, misdemeanors. Soon she was watching movies that were definitely not spiritually uplifting. Unbeknownst to Carly, the girl who had previously occupied the dorm room she was in had been involved in spiritualism. Even though the girl was no longer at the school, the spirits had not moved on.

Soon, Carly saw shadows that shouldn't have been there. She began hearing voices that would tell her to do things she didn't want to do. When she refused to do their bidding, the voices became more aggressive. She could sense an evil presence in her room.

For a long time, Carly didn't tell anyone what was happening to her, but her friends noticed strange things about Carly's behavior. She would be staring off and seeing things they didn't see. She could see a huge figure staring at her. She felt as if time had stopped. She was very scared but didn't know how to get help. She would close her eyes, and the figure would be gone.

Finally, the pressure of these experiences forced her to talk with the associate dean of the girl's dorm. The dean said, "If this happens to you again, come to me or my dad [the science teacher], and we will pray with you. In fact, we will anoint the room you are staying in to remove the devil and his agents from the building."

Carly's room was the only student room in the basement of the dormitory. One night, Carly was in bed and heard the usual room check-up the head dean did at 10:30 at night. The head dean, who lived up the road, checked the room, walked out the door, and drove away. Carly could hear it all.

Suddenly, Carly felt afraid. Someone was walking down the hallway, and she knew it was not the head dean. No hallway door had opened. The footsteps then came to Carly's door and stopped. She heard the door handle rattle as someone was attempting to open her door.

With great fear in her heart, Carly prayed, "God, please help me!" She knew it was an evil presence at her door. After Carly prayed, the jiggling of the door handle stopped. But soon she heard screams, blood-curdling screams. Then gunshots and more screams. Terrified, Carly wondered what she should do. Should she go to help whoever was hurt or should she stay in her room? Finally, she decided to stay in her room.

The next morning, Carly asked the other dorm girls if they had heard anything during the night. None had heard a thing. Now Carly knew she was being harassed by demons, so she again approached the assistant dean for help.

"Do you have anything in your room that is connected to Satan in any way?" the dean asked.

"Well, I have this deck of cards I shouldn't have in my room."

"Okay. Go get them, and we'll burn them now."

The cards were burned, and the demonic harassment stopped. Carly knew that Fairhaven had the faculty that could help her with any spiritual problem that came her way. She now began to fully understand why God had directed her to Fairhaven Academy.

Carly grew spiritually and learned to rely on God's Word for encouragement and strength. Isaiah 65:1–5 were especially meaningful to her when she seemed alone and isolated. The Lord says, "…I am found of them that sought Me not…." Carly knows one thing: Our Father in heaven cares about her, and He has pursued her even when she was not looking for Him. He is there to shield her from the evil one, and He is always present to help her in her time of need. God has become her very special Friend, and this is the result of many prayers offered on her behalf!

CHAPTER 9

A CHILD UNATTENDED

There are times when parents trust their children to play in other rooms with family, friends, or relatives. Unfortunately, the devil watches for opportunities to corrupt young minds. That is exactly what happened to Jason, a carefully raised Adventist boy. However, his story has a happy ending that will make you smile.

*****

"Psst!" Jason's cousin nodded his head towards the closet. "Come over here. I want to show you something." Slowly, cousin Jack opened the closet door to reveal stacks of comic books with eye-catching covers. "Help yourself. We can read these here, and no one will ever know."

Jason's eyes grew wide as he sorted through the colorful comics. It was Sabbath afternoon, and his parents were visiting with his aunt and uncle in the living room. The boys had been left to play in his cousin's bedroom.

What a treat to read the exciting comics since he had never seen such things before! This kind of reading had not been allowed in his home.

Soon the afternoon sped by, and his mom called that they were ready to go home. Jason's interest had been aroused, and his thoughts on the trip home were on those exciting comic books. That week, in his public school, Jason heard his classmates talk about the hilarious cartoons they watched on television last Saturday morning. As they talked, a desire to enter their world began to grow in Jason's heart. After all, the comics were great to read, and the cartoons must be even more fun.

Jason's home always began and ended the Sabbath with worship time. He remembers sensing God's presence in his life as a young child, and one sermon, when he was about eight years of age, really impressed him. The sermon emphasized that God is stronger than Satan, and young Jason believed it. Going to the boy's bathroom, he said out loud, "I bet Satan doesn't even know my name."

Outside the bathroom window a voice called, "Jason!"

This experience frightened him and helped him realized there must be a supernatural world to contend with.

From the fourth through the tenth grades, Jason attended Adventist schools, but he felt that he was not strongly influenced spiritually during that time. Occasionally, he would hear a sermon that spoke to his heart, but, as he and his friends continued to live a forbidden lifestyle, the effect of these sermons disappeared. Because he had learned the Adventist culture, Jason looked the part of a good Adventist boy, and he continued to go to church only because he knew it would break his parents' hearts if he refused to go with them.

This led to Jason's life becoming a double life. Video games, movies, television, all contributed to his lack of spiritual interest, but the leading factor that made him decide to withdraw from the church was a Death Metal Band. Being a musician, he loved the technicality this band displayed as they produced ear-shattering music. Some of the band members were extremely talented musicians, and the music was decidedly hypnotic. As Jason interacted with these young men, some of whom openly declared themselves to be Satanists, he realized he was living the life of Judas. He was appearing to be a Christian, but he loved everything the devil had to offer in his heart. So, Jason made a decision: he would leave God and everything God represented behind.

Once this decision was made, Jason wrote a detailed letter to the church board asking that his name be removed as a church member. He was explicit in requesting that no one contact him to persuade him to come back, and he stated he no longer believed in God. The church board responded they would respect his decision, but they would continue to pray for him.

The years passed. Five years, ten years, thirteen years, and all this time Jason's parents and the church faithfully continued to pray for him, and the Holy Spirit faithfully worked to reach Jason's heart. Jason tells the step-by-step process when this happened:

> I was working at McDonald's, and two Jehovah Witnesses entered the building and began to talk with me about God. I started to laugh at them in my mind. "You don't know who you're talking to," I told them. "I am a Satanist!"
>
> But even as I was saying this the Holy Spirit said to me, "You know what the Truth is!" Eventually, I lost interest in Satanism. It was boring. It was another religion which told you to do whatever you want to do. Then, I had a kind of falling out with the Death Metal Band. I quit listening to satanic music, but the devil wasn't through with me yet. I became obsessed with the video game called World of Warcraft. I played this game for hours on end and built multiple characters in this virtual world. Then someone hacked my account and sold everything I owned for cash. All of this made me consider how I had spent all those years for nothing, so I was done with the video game world after that.
>
> Now I played pool and spent time in bars. How many times the Lord must have protected me as I drove home drunk! One of the girls I met in a bar was heavily into horror stories, and, as a result, I began listening to all of Stephen King's horror books on audiobooks. The Harry Potter series as well as other horror stories occupied much of my time. Soon, I wanted to write my own horror stories, and it gave me the feeling of power to think dark thoughts. But then there came a change.

Jason went to live with his parents, and he reached out to his friend, Andrew, who lived in Texas. Andrew believed in God and helped Jason begin to seriously think about his spiritual condition. After having given up drinking alcohol and drugs, one night, as Jason was sleeping, he had a horrible dream. He was being pushed to murder someone and he prayed,

"Jesus, help me not to do this." The person he was to murder turned to him with a demonic face.

When he woke up, he tried to pray, but he couldn't talk. He felt his whole body vibrate as if he were next to a helicopter. Once he finally was able to speak, an audible voice tried to override his prayer, but as he prayed, he felt a peace and warmth come over him. Jason states that he has never felt closer to God than in those moments.

Soon after this demonic attack, Jason loaded every spiritualistic book he owned, took them to his workplace, and dumped them in the garbage bin. After that, the attacks diminished and stopped. Satan had been conquered.

Jason is now a leader in his local Adventist church. He has strong opinions about staying away from anything that has to do with the devil, for his experiences have convinced him of the reality of the spiritual warfare that exists all around us. And his step-by-step, complete surrender to the Lord, though it took thirteen years, was the result of the consistent prayers of those who love him and God's power to save those in Satan's grasp. What a mighty God we serve!

CHAPTER 10

TWO KINDS OF MOTHERS

Children grow up in many different kinds of homes. Some are peaceful and orderly while others are chaotic and disturbing. The next two stories tell of two homes that were opposite in atmosphere and how God overruled in each situation. These stories bring much comfort to those who are overwhelmed with their present circumstances. Remember, God is still on His throne, and the prayers of His saints are heard.

> *These stories bring much comfort to those who are overwhelmed with their present circumstances.*

*****

Paul, the youngest of three children, grew up in a humble home during the Great Depression. The Depression caused his family to lose almost everything. Paul's mother raised flowers to make wreaths, and she baked bread and cookies to provide some sort of income for the family. Their family was short of food. If they had milk to drink, it was because a church member brought it every other week to the house. Without an icebox or refrigerator, the milk didn't last long, so it was a real treat to get it at least every two weeks.

In spite of the lack of food, Paul's childhood was pleasant. His mother was a Seventh-day Adventist as a result of a colporteur coming through their community when she was fourteen years old, and her parents and her three brothers also became Adventists. Paul's father was a fine Lutheran man who had the habit of smoking. Twenty five years passed before he gave up smoking and became a Seventh-day Adventist as well.

Paul describes his boyhood home as low-key, moderate, and very earnest. Paul's mother made sure the baths were taken, the shoes were shined, the clothes were ironed, and the house was sparkling clean before the Sabbath began on Friday evening. All the food was fixed before the sun went down. She was faithful in her tithing and Sabbath observance, and Paul remembers them reading *Review and Herald*, an Adventist magazine, on the Sabbath.

The elementary school years had an impact on Paul's thinking. While in grades three to five, Paul was taught in church school by an Adventist lady. Later in high school, his older sister raised the money for Paul to attend Auburn Adventist Academy. His experiences at both schools were positive and would influence decisions he made much later in life.

Eventually, Paul attended the College of Medical Evangelists, presently known as Loma Linda University. During this time, from ages twenty to thirty, Paul attended church occasionally. Soon his practice grew, and he became busier and busier. As his responsibilities grew, he was simply too tired to go to church. Eventually, Paul married a non-Adventist woman who did not encourage him to attend church on the Sabbath. During this time, however, Paul continued to believe all the Adventist doctrines. In fact, he states he never had any doubt about what he had learned as a child.

Occasionally, Paul's mother would say, "Paul, you need to come back to church." And, probably to satisfy his mother, he would attend church. He says he very seldom attended church all those years past his thirties. Paul's mother lived to be one hundred and eleven years of age, and during those years, she would pray that her youngest child would return to church. She passed away without seeing the answer to her prayers.

Time went on. One day, when Paul was in his late seventies, his wife entered the house and cried, "Something just bit me on the neck. I really don't feel good."

Paul thought, *Uh oh. I'd better get my medical bag!*

Hurrying back, he reached his wife but not in time to give her an injection to counteract the anaphylactic shock. His wife died as he reached for the syringe.

Now, life took a much different turn for Paul. Consumed with grief, he came to church to seek comfort and encouragement. Reconnecting with like believers and hearing truth, once again, inspired Paul to continue meeting with God's people on the Sabbath day. As long as his health permitted, he was a regularly attending member.

Who is the hero in this story? Obviously, it was because of the Holy Spirit's work that Paul eventually came back to the Lord. And this was because of a faithful mother's prayers, who was a great exemplar of praying in faith. A mother who refused to give up praying, even though for many decades and until her last breath, she saw no results. What a reunion in heaven that will be when she sees Paul enter the golden gates. Praise God for faithful, praying mothers!

*****

Sometimes, the mother has never been introduced to our Savior and actively works against the promptings of the Holy Spirit. Rachel's story will inspire you with hope for those who have grown up in homes without Jesus.

*****

"We don't serve God in this house!" Rachel's mother screamed, her voice rising with each syllable. "And don't you ever come back here again!" Young Rachel stared wide-eyed as the two Jehovah Witnesses beat a very hasty retreat down the sidewalk and out the front gate. "Don't you ever go to church," Rachel felt the intensity of her mother's words. "They are a bunch of hypocrites and very judgmental."

Life for young Rachel was full of family turmoil and anti-God sentiments, and His name was used only in profanity. By age twelve, Rachel's mother introduced her to methamphetamine, and the chains of drug addiction wound tighter and tighter around this young woman as the years sped by.

In spite of her mother's warning never to go to church, Rachel did have some contact with churches. A schoolmate's parents insisted that Rachel attend their church if she was going to stay overnight with their daughter, so Rachel went, but she found the experience to be unfriendly and uninteresting. The few times she went to an Adventist church, however, she enjoyed the visit because the people were friendly, and she always came away with a small present or a book.

Later, Rachel married her childhood sweetheart, Casey. They had known each other since the fifth grade, and their lives together were extremely secular. It involved alcohol, cigarettes, drugs, and filthy language that, Rachel says, "Would make a sailor blush."

When their daughter decided to move out of their home because of differences with her mother, Rachel became depressed and jumped into the drug world completely, staying there until 2019. She became so physically affected by her drug intake that Casey felt sure she would die if she continued to abuse her body. Because of this, he quit his truck-driving job to stay at home to protect Rachel from drugs, and he began to attend an Adventist church with his mother. As he urged Rachel to attend church with him, she resisted thinking, "He's trying to cram religion down my throat." Eventually, Rachel promised that they would read a devotional together each day. Casey, wisely, insisted that she read the book out loud to him while he ate. After he had gone to work, out of curiosity, Rachel would look up texts in the Bible.

Finally, Rachel went to church with Casey even though she was intoxicated and felt very uncomfortable there because of her condition. All this time, Casey and others were praying earnestly for her. Casey was so earnest about his wife's salvation that he quit work for five days to pray for her. During those days off, he followed Rachel around telling her how much he loved her and how much God loved her.

Thanksgiving night, Rachel and Casey went to their garage and dropped to their knees. Rachel was at a tipping point. "I can't stop taking meth, and I'm going to die from a heart attack. I need help!"

With that realization, Rachel entered a rehabilitation program that lasted for four months. Faithful Casey accompanied her on every visit, even sleeping in the lobby when necessary. When the program was completed, Rachel knew her spiritual life was a disaster, and she told her husband, "I want to come to church with you." Entering the Sabbath School room, she heard the teacher tell of his experiences when waking up every morning. He explained that even before he lifted his head from the pillow, he would ask Jesus to be with him for that day. That small bit of advice rang a bell in Rachel's mind, and she determined to make this her practice.

Desiring to know about the Bible, Rachel and Casey asked the pastor to study with them, and during these studies, the pastor prayed for help for her addiction issues. After praying for two days, Rachel had no more desire for drugs. However, smoking was still an issue. On her way to surgery, Rachel prayed for the Lord to take away her desire for cigarettes. Three days after coming home from surgery, she went to the garage to smoke, lit the cigarette, and inhaled. It was awful! From that point on, Rachel did not smoke another cigarette.

The path has not been easy since Rachel made the decision to follow God. The devil has attacked her physically more than once, but she reminds herself, "God will clear the way for you." Prayer opened the door for God's Spirit to break the chains of drug use, smoking, alcohol, and swearing in Rachel's life. She will tell you, emphatically, that our Father in heaven is infinitely more powerful than anything the devil can throw at us. Rachel knows. She has experienced God's power and has been unshackled.

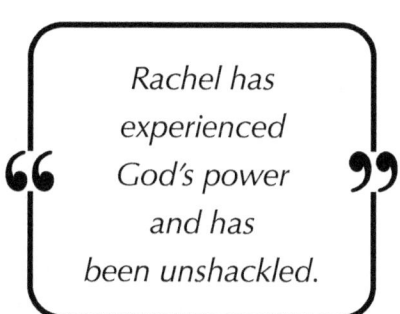

Rachel has experienced God's power and has been unshackled.

CHAPTER 11

GOD'S FAITHFUL PROVISIONS

The story of the widow of Zarephath in 1 Kings 17 is amazing. Elijah, the Lord's prophet, had delivered an unpopular message to King Ahab. There would be no more rain or dew until Elijah announced the return of moisture. Israel had fallen so low that they were involved in degraded heathen practices, so the Lord had to get their attention. Hence, no more rain.

Because Ahab's anger was so predictable, God told Elijah to go to the brook Cherith where he had plenty of water, and ravens delivered bread and flesh to the prophet in the morning and bread and flesh in the evening. After a while, the brook dried up. The Lord then told Elijah to go to Zarephath where God had commanded a widow to take Elijah into her home and to feed him.

Arriving in Zarephath, the prophet soon saw a thin woman gathering sticks to make a cooking fire. Their conversation looked something like this:

"Please get me a drink of water," pleaded the prophet. She turned to grant his request. "Also, get me a morsel of bread to eat."

At this plea for food, the widow declined. "I have only a handful of meal and a little oil to make for me and my son. After we eat it, we will die."

"Don't worry," the prophet assured her. "Make me a little cake first. Then make a cake for you and your son, for the Lord has said the barrel of meal shall not waste neither shall the cruse of oil fail until the Lord sends rain on the earth."

This courageous woman did as the prophet requested, and his word was true. Neither she nor her son nor Elijah were hungry during the years of that terrible drought because God provided the meal and the oil every day (see 1 Kings 17:1–16).

Now, that's a fantastic story! Imagine going to your pantry every day to find enough food for the next day, miraculously planted by angel hands. It would be a story to tell your friends and relatives, wouldn't it? But does our Father in heaven repeat miracles of this magnitude in our day and age? Well, read Manuel and Consuela's story and then draw your conclusions.

*****

Manuel entered the house quietly. How could he tell Consuela he had not found work today? Soon he heard Consuela's sweet voice.

"Hola, Manuel. How did it go today?" The happy lilt of her voice quickly changed when she saw Manuel's downcast face. "Oh, sweetheart. What's wrong?"

Manuel sat down on the wooden chair next to the table. "I didn't find work today. All the farms have all the help they need. I'll try again tomorrow. By the way, how much food do we have?"

Consuela quickly moved to the flour bin and the bean pot. "It looks like we have enough for one more day. Sweetheart, God will provide. He always has in the past, and He will take care of us." Her voice was full of confidence and courage. "Besides, look how the Lord has blessed us since we've decided to follow Him."

Manuel nodded his head. He knew his darling wife was right. They had always found work as field workers since coming from Mexico. Their lives had been so blessed since listening to the biblical truths presented by an evangelist. He taught them about the seventh-day Sabbath, the second coming of Jesus, and what happens to people when they die. So many truths Manuel and Consuela had absorbed as the evangelist led them from one Bible text to another. It all fit together like a wonderful puzzle, but it was challenging to empty the freezer of pork when they learned the health principles God had given in His word.

Manuel and Consuela lived from paycheck to paycheck and throwing away all that frozen pork was a real test of faith for them. However, they were overwhelmed with peace as they step-by-step attempted to follow God's word. But now this. No work.

Early the next morning, Manuel rose before the sun was up and prepared to leave. He knew there might be vacancies in the work force at the farms, which he could fill if he was the first to arrive. Spending a few moments for worship, he kissed his sleepy wife good-bye and hopped into his old, trusty truck.

Driving to the first farm, he inquired about work for the day only to be told no more workers were needed. As he drove from farm to farm, he prayed, "Lord, help me find work," but the story was the same. Each farm had adequate workers and his help was not needed. Finally, after spending the day searching for employment, Manuel turned towards home. How could he tell Consuela, once again, that he had not found work?

As he drove into the driveway and turned off the old pick-up, he hesitated to get out. After all, they would not be able to buy groceries today, and this was the last day their food supplies could hold out. Entering the house, he attempted to put on a brave face as Consuela ran to meet him.

"Did you find work today?" Her eyes searched his face.

"No, Consuela, no work today."

"Well," she assured him, "We have tortillas and beans to eat today, so let's sit down and enjoy dinner. Remember, sweetheart, God will provide."

As they ate dinner, Manuel wished his faith were as strong as his wife's, yet, deep inside, he knew God would provide. "By the way," he turned to Consuela, "how much food do we have left?"

Looking in the food bins, Consuela said, "It seems strange, but it looks like we have enough for one more day."

And so it was, as the days passed, Manuel could not find work, yet each time he returned home to deliver the sad news, Consuela told him they had food for one more day. This story repeated itself for thirty days until Manuel found work once again! Yes, our Father in heaven provided thirty miracles to show His dear children His care for their well-being.

Manuel told this story in a Sabbath School class in southern Oregon several years later, testifying that our God watches over His own. It is a fact;

God's Word is true, and He is still performing miracles for those who are faithful to Him. Praise His holy name!

*****

Printer ink jets never run out of ink. Wrong!

Printer ink jets sometimes run out of ink. Wrong!

Printer ink jets always run out of ink. Right, unless aided by a hand from heaven above. Jonathon and his family have an amazing story to tell of God's help in their time of need.

> *Printers always run out of ink, unless aided by a hand from heaven.*

*****

Jonathon and his family were living in Berrien Springs, Michigan, while he was working on a master's degree in theology at Andrew's University. Jonathon and his wife determined to live as frugally as possible, so they sacrificed in many areas. They realized that the money they had saved in the bank would be needed after graduation, and, not wanting the indebtedness of student loans they would have to face later on, they decided to find odd jobs and to live as prudently as they could. This included even not enjoying the luxury of heat in their small home during the bitter Michigan winters, so they opted to wear snowsuits while they were at home. Life was being lived at a bare minimum.

One day, Jonathon was printing an assignment, which was soon to be due for one of his classes. Many of his assignments were twenty to thirty pages long, and much ink and paper was used in the process. Looking at the weak printing on the last page printed, Jonathon realized the ink jet was soon to be depleted. The printer read, "Low ink."

Going to his wife, he asked, "What shall we do? This paper is due soon, and we simply can't afford to buy a new ink jet."

"I don't know except we're going to have to pray about it," her voice showed concern.

"Okay. Then let's pray. Dear Father in heaven," Jonathon had a pleading tone, "You know how we've tried to live so carefully to stay out of debt. The ink cartridge is about to give out, and we simply can't afford to buy a new one. So, since I know that You can do anything, I'm asking you to keep the printer printing. I have many papers that will be due, and I need good quality printing, so please honor my request, if it is Your will. Thank You. Amen"

"Well, we'll just have to rely on God and see what happens." Jonathon's voice had more courage now.

Going back to the computer, Jonathon hit "print" once again. Immediately, the printer sprung to life, and a picture perfect paper fell to the floor.

That's amazing! Jonathon thought. *I wonder if it's just a fluke performance.* Again, he hit the "print" button and another perfect paper fell to the floor.

"Honey, look what's happening! I believe my prayer is being answered!" And it was. For months and months, the ink cartridge, which had signaled it was low, continued to print beautiful papers.

Near the end of his tenure at Andrews University, Jonathon's aunt and uncle came for a visit. "Come see this amazing printer!" Jonathon was anxious to show them the miracle of the same ink jet that produced hundreds of pages for his class work. When the aunt and uncle learned of Jonathon's financial plight, they bought ink jets and many reams of paper and left them on Jonathon's doorstep before they left town.

Once again, Jonathon tried to print with the old ink jet, but the printer would not print! God had met his need as long as there was a need. Now, he no longer needed the ink, and the amazing miracle stopped. This faith-building experience would never be forgotten by Jonathon or his family, and it is a faith-builder for others to realize our God is able to do more than what we ask or think. After all, supplying ink to an ink jet would be no trick at all for one of His angels.

CHAPTER 12

TRUSTING GOD'S TIMING

We all desire immediate and direct answers to our prayers, and are tempted to become discouraged when the answer is delayed or comes in an unlooked-for form. But God is too wise and good to answer our prayers always at just the time and in just the manner we desire. He will do more and better for us than to accomplish all our wishes. And because we can trust His wisdom and love, we should not ask Him to concede to our will, but should seek to enter into and accomplish His purpose. Our desires and interest should be lost in His will. These experiences that test faith are for our benefit…Faith is strengthened by exercise. We must let patience have its perfect work, remembering that there are precious promises in the Scriptures for those who wait upon the Lord. (*Ministry of Healing*, p. 230)

Don's experience with his lost keys definitely increased his faith. Here is his story in his own words:

*****

I had been principal of Red Mountain Adventist Academy in Salem, Oregon, for the past twelve years and had come to the end of another school year. As is always the case when working with people, that spring had seen several interpersonal issues to which I, as a principal, had tried to bring resolution for the parties involved. Certain students were not getting along with other students, a parent was unhappy with a teacher, and there was one staff issue. I had been praying to God for several months, asking Him to solve these issues between people. Now the school year had ended, but none of these issues had been resolved.

The summer had come, and quiet and peace settled over the school campus. I missed the students being there, but I did accomplish a lot more of the items on my checklist when working in my office. I got in my blue Chevy pick-up and headed for home in the afternoon, planning to work on one of my home projects. I had to get the truck hide-a-key out in order to drive home since I had lost my keys to the truck about six months ago. This was somewhat embarrassing to me as I usually know where all of my things are while other family members are more likely to misplace things from time to time.

At home, I changed into my work clothes and went to the garage where my table saw sat. The project that I was building required lumber that was narrower than what I had, so I was going to rip it to the correct width on the table saw. As I ran wood through the saw, I began talking to God about the issues at the school that I had been asking Him to solve for me. Over the years I have gotten better about talking to God not just at "prayer time" but whenever issues rose to my mind that I needed to bring to Him.

In my frustration that these issues between people had not been resolved in the last couple of months, I began to "chew on God's ear" about them. Fortunately, God is big enough that He can take it even when you chew on His ear in frustration. I told Him that I was not happy that He had not resolved these issues when I had been asking Him to for several months now. In my frustration I said, "And I have been asking You to tell me where my truck keys are for the last six months, and You have not shown me!" The moment those words came out of my mouth, something happened. I immediately dropped the piece of wood that I was running through the table saw, walked twenty feet across the garage floor, lifted up a small piece of insulation that was left over from insulating the garage walls, and picked up my truck keys. It was like I had become a robot. I never heard an audible voice, but, obviously, God had spoken to me.

God had given me the irrefutable proof that while the issues at school had not been resolved, he had heard my prayers. He was working in my life and in my school, and he wanted me to know it. Looking back on it, I realize that in the next few days and weeks, I became proud that God had done this for me. Then I came to the understanding that God only needs to do something like that for someone whose faith in Him has weakened. Picture Elijah after Mount Carmel in the desert wishing to die, when God comes and does another miracle for him. Picture Jacob struggling with God through a whole night. Picture John the Baptist in Herod's prison.

At this point, I know one thing. I do not need to become frustrated when my prayers are not answered immediately or even in a little while. God asks me to trust Him and know that He hears my prayers and will bring solutions to my requests in His good time. He asks me to persist in prayer, even if answers seem to take a long time. I believe that God will never again need to do something like this for me to strengthen my faith. I know that He is there every moment of every day and always intervening in my life for my best good.

> *I do not need to become frustrated when my prayers are not answered immediately.*

*****

It took time for Don's prayers to be answered, but his faith was increased in spite of the wait. At other times, our Father in heaven chooses to answer quickly for the good of all those involved. Jerry needed help immediately!

*****

Jerry walked to the back of the house and analyzed the kidney-bean shaped swimming pool under the trees. The owner had said the pH of the pool was not correct. Something was wrong. *It must be the chemical feeder is needing fixing,* Jerry thought, as he looked for the hose leading to the pool's water. The pool cleaning business he had started had done well in the past several months, and summertime was the busiest for him. However, life looked a little precarious since baby Joel's premature birth two months before. His complicated delivery had necessitated extra medical attention, and Joel was placed in ICU for two months. Jerry's high deductible insurance had refused to pay the extra fees, and the hospital bill had soared to $90,000. It was all so overwhelming! With four babies at home under the age of five and the additional debt of the medical bill, Jerry knew his pool business needed to flourish to meet all the needs of his growing family.

Stepping to the side of the pool, Jerry lifted the main device that delivered chemicals to the pool. As he twisted the end cap, suddenly the hose broke, and chemicals shot out covering his left eye. The pain was excruciating! Covering his eye, Jerry ran to a faucet and began washing his eye with water for thirty minutes until it became unbearable to wash it anymore. There was no relief. Quickly calling his wife, Jerry managed to explain what had happened. Jessica, his wife, was horrified, and after putting all four babies into the car, she sped to the address where Jerry had been working.

Dr. Laurie Chen, a local ophthalmologist, was busily tending to the forty patients that had been scheduled for that day. A staff member entered the room. "Jerry Jenson is here needing attention for his eye. Can you fit him into your schedule today?" Knowing that her schedule was packed, Dr. Chen made to the decision to fit Jerry in anyway because he and Jessica were personal friends of hers. Not knowing the seriousness of Jerry's injury, she continued to tend to the patient at hand.

Finally, going to the waiting room, Dr. Chen saw Jerry sitting quietly with hands over both eyes. His face was very red. Helping Jerry into the examining room, Dr. Chen took one look at the damaged eye and realized Jerry was in very serious trouble. The entire cornea of his left eye was white. It was opaque! There was an area where the skin had sloughed off. The cornea under the top and bottom of the eyelids was necrotic.

Jerry wasn't sure what kind of chemical had splashed into his eye, an acid or base chemical. He thought probably concentrated bleach or muriatic acid. Dr. Chen knew his eye had a better chance if the chemical was acidic.

After putting numbing drops in the eye, Dr. Chen carefully pulled away the dead tissue for the next ten to fifteen minutes. It was the consistency of plastic. After removing skin, Dr. Chen saw Jerry's eye's red blood vessels appeared to be intact, which she realized was a good sign, but she also knew that removing all this dead skin would greatly increase Jerry's potential for infection to his eye.

After doing all she could, Dr. Chen walked to her office to call a specialist who had dealt with chemical burns to the eye. When she explained the details, he replied, "You know, Dr. Chen, after you do everything you can do, there is little hope for this man's eye."

"I know," she replied. "I know."

Returning to the examining room, Dr. Chen prescribed pain medication and antibiotics for Jerry and asked him to come the next day for her to check his progress.

The next day, the doctor found the eyelid fused to the eye ball. Once again, carefully separating the eyelid from the cornea, she knew there was little hope for normal vision for Jerry. However, she did have a plan to keep the eyelid from fusing to his eye again. The office had one ring, which, when fitted around the eye, would prevent the skin from adhering to Jerry's eyeball. But she needed two rings, so she called the company's representative to see what could be worked out. She explained Jerry's family's financial situation, the high deductible insurance, and asked if the representative could help. He kindly worked on this and sent two rings for very little cost. (They were usually around $1,200 each. Jerry's high deductible insurance would not have helped pay for the rings.)

Meanwhile, Jerry's entire church was praying, and by Friday evening, two days after Jerry's accident, the church pastor and elders joined together around Jerry's bed to anoint him. The Bible counsels, "Is any sick among you? let him call for the elders of the church; and let them pray over him, anointing him with oil in the name of the Lord. And the prayer of faith shall save the sick, and the Lord shall raise him up; and if he have committed sins, they shall be forgiven him" (James 5:14, 15).

A small amount of olive oil was placed on Jerry's forehead as the church pastor and the elders asked for forgiveness of their sins and Jerry's sins. They then asked for Jerry's eye to be healed, if it was within God's will to do so, knowing that our Father in heaven has an overview of each one's life and knows what is best.

From the day of the anointing, Jerry's eye began to heal very quickly. Daily, Dr. Chen saw improvement in his eye, and in two weeks, Jerry had 20/20 vision in the injured eye. Against all odds, the blind eye began to function. Jerry says there is some cloudiness in his left eye, but he is able to function normally. Both he and Dr. Chen know that God's hand intervened in his life to prevent blindness. Financial and physical miracles had happened very quickly, one after another. Once again, our Father in heaven heard the prayers of His people and interceded for one of His faithful children.

CHAPTER 13

THE PROMISE

Are you a single male who is sometimes lonely and wishes you could find a lady with whom you could serve the Lord? Proverbs 18:22 makes an interesting statement: "Whoso findeth a wife findeth a good thing, and obtaineth favour of the LORD." Jeff claimed the promise of Proverbs 18:22, but he knew that in order for God to hear his prayer, he must put away anything in his life that he knew was offensive to God. After that, he was faithful in claiming the promise every day. The results Jeff experienced will encourage you to follow the same conditions and to claim that promise as well. Our Father in heaven wants to bless our lives with much happiness. In order for Him to do that, we must simply cooperate with Him.

*****

The phone rang as Jeff sat in the living room of his condominium.

"Hi, Jeff!" It was the familiar voice of his sister, Allie. She had a special sparkle in her voice this evening. "Say, Jeff, there's a girl here in Colorado we'd like you to meet. She's very nice, quite a bit younger than you, but you know, love can reach all bounds. Why don't you come on back, and we'll introduce you to her." Allie's enthusiasm was evident even over the phone.

"Aw, I don't know, Allie. I've dated so many women, and the dating scene gets old after a while. I'm simply not meeting the right woman for me. I'll think about it, but, right now, I'm not terribly excited about the prospect of being disappointed again." Jeff's voice had a flat effect.

"Well, think about it," Allie urged. "We've gotten to know her, and we like her. You might enjoy meeting her just to network. You can meet her friends and vice versa. I know it's hard once you're out of school to find suitable people to date, but give it some thought. You might really like her."

"Thanks, sis. I may make the trip back just to see you and your family. Anyway, I appreciate you thinking of me."

In time, Jeff made the trip to Colorado and agreed with his sister that her friend was a nice gal. They met again in California, but Jeff knew, once again, this was not the one for him. His prayers became more earnest. "Lord, I'm tired of living alone. I need someone to talk to, to love. It would be great to have children. At thirty-four years old, my prospects are dwindling. Please help me."

One Sabbath, an announcement was made at church for an upcoming evangelistic meeting conducted by Pastor Glen Coon. Jeff's attention was drawn to the dates they would be held, and soon he found himself enjoying the ABCs of Prayer meetings, which Pastor Coon presented in such a dramatic way. "Just *Ask* the Lord for something you know will be within His will, *Believe* He will answer you, and *Claim* the promise that will be answered." As Jeff listened, he found himself wondering if this could apply to looking for a wife.

After one meeting, Jeff approached the rostrum where Pastor Coon was talking with church members. Finally, he found an opportunity to speak.

"I don't have much time to talk with you," the pastor said, "but tell me in five minutes what you need, and I'll try to help you.

"I'm looking for a wife," Jeff's voice betrayed his loneliness.

"All right," the pastor responded. "Make sure you meet the conditions, such as putting sin out of your life, and open your Bible to Proverbs 18:22. It says, "Whoso findeth a wife findeth a good thing, and obtaineth favour of the LORD." Put your finger on that text every day asking, believing, and claiming God's promise. Within one year you will either be engaged or married."

"Thank you, sir. I will do that."

The days rolled by with Jeff faithfully following the pastor's direction. A few weeks later, he received a call from the new school teacher who had just arrived in the area. She needed help in the earliteen department at the church, and his name and phone number was one of several she had been given as possibilities for other adults who could assist her. Something happened during that phone call. They talked and talked and talked and talked. For three and a half hours they talked. Eventually, they began dating, and, yes, within a year they were engaged.

A divine appointment? Absolutely! This couple has been married for fifty years, and they have three children and thirteen grandchildren. Our Father in heaven directed Eliezer to find a wife for Isaac, and, if it is within His providential will, He will do the same today. Remove sin from your life and Ask, Believe, and Claim the promises found in His book. Our God is very, very faithful to each one of us! Just ask Jeff.

CHAPTER 14

IMPOSSIBLE GOALS

M any times, we have goals or dreams that seem impossible to be realized. Such was the case of Augustin. However, Psalms 37:4, 5 promises, "Delight thyself also in the LORD: and he shall give thee the desires of thine heart. Commit thy way unto the LORD; trust also in him; and he shall bring it to pass." Augustin had been taught to commit his ways to God, and God did amazing things for him!

*****

Augustin patted the head of his dog and leaned back against the tree to think, once again, about what the future might hold for him. Life had been good to Augustin. His very devout Adventist family lived in Chile, and while they were not wealthy by worldly standards, all their basic needs had been met, and it was a happy home. *I should be content,* Augustin thought as he looked at the sky. *But somehow I dream of being a doctor. How could that be possible considering my family isn't wealthy? How can that dream become a reality?*

Then Augustin thought of Dr. Ben Carson's story. Dr. Carson's mother cleaned houses for a living, and he did not have a father in his life. That man had risen from a humble beginning to greatness because of his mother's prayers. *Well,* Augustin thought, *I'll pray about it, and if it is God's will, my dream to enter medicine will come true.*

And pray he did. He knew that God is not limited by circumstances and could arrange all the details for him to reach his goal. Augustin's determination to be a doctor was unusual, considering the attitudes of the boys in his small town. Most of them simply wanted to be on the soccer team, but Augustin's parents valued education and they supported his dream.

Time went by, and, eventually, Augustin took tests to enter the nearest university. He knew the competition would be fierce since it was difficult to get into this school, but he was accepted, and after four years, he graduated. Now the next step. After applying to medical school and receiving his admission, Augustin was very happy to spend the time and effort it took to successfully learn the principles of medicine. In the back of his mind, however, he sensed that God had further plans for him. He knew medical missionary work was important, but he wasn't sure how to integrate the spiritual component into his medical practice.

Life for doctors in Chile is good, and most doctors stay there and enjoy the good life their profession affords them. Augustin, however, had different thoughts. He wanted to get to the United States for a residency program in internal medicine, so he prayed and prayed this would happen. Unbeknownst to Augustin, his mother was praying the opposite prayer. She did not feel he was ready to go to the United States, so she consistently prayed the doors to the United States would stay shut.

And stay shut they did. After medical school, Augustin worked in an emergency room and enjoyed working there when, out of the blue, an invitation came to attend a medical missionary course at Clear Valley Institute in Georgia, USA. *How can this happen?* Augustin questioned. *I don't have a passport, and I don't speak English.* But as he prayed, everything came together, and in 2018, he found himself flying to Georgia to attend their training course.

After the training course at Clear Valley, Augustin flew back to Chile to continue his job. But in December of 2018, Clear Valley called and explained their medical missionary course coordinator would be leaving and asked if he would consider volunteering as the coordinator for the time being. As Augustin wrestled with this decision, his father told him, "You've always wanted to serve God as a medical missionary." And so, the scale was tipped. Augustin quit his job in Chile and approached the United States Embassy for a visa to the USA. At this point, Augustin told the Lord, "I surrender all my plans to You. Whatever you want is what I will do." In one month's time, all the necessary documents came together, and Augustin saw God's hand at work. He knew he was to go to Clear Valley Institute.

As a volunteer at Clear Valley, he had no income, and there was very little time to study for a residency program. Somehow, in the midst of his busy days, Augustin found time to study, found the money to apply for a residency, and was coached on how to apply for a residency by doctors connected with Clear Valley. His contact with doctors from all over the world was just one of the great benefits Augustin enjoyed as he volunteered one year at Clear Valley. Another benefit became evident as he became very proficient in English.

During the heavy schedule of that year, Augustin applied to sixty-five residency programs all over the United States. In his heart, however, he wanted to do a program at an Adventist hospital. *It's all in God's hands now,* he reminded himself.

After attending an AMEN (Adventist Medical Evangelism Network) conference where he interacted with many Adventist doctors, he received an invitation to interview for a residency at Kettering Medical Center (an Adventist hospital). Because his visa was expiring, he returned to Chile in February 2020, and then the pandemic hit. However, in March 2020, Augustin was accepted into the internal medicine residency program at Kettering Medical Center.

Now much more paperwork was needed because of the pandemic, but God's hand was over it all. Augustin received an emergency passport and visa in the same day. Many flights were cancelled due to the pandemic restrictions, but every flight from Chile to Dayton, Ohio, were on schedule, and Augustin made it to Kettering without a hitch.

He is now in his second year of residency and knows, without a doubt, that God has led this young Chilean boy with a big dream step-by-step, through many seemingly impossible situations, to the realization of that dream. Praise God for His goodness to His children!

*****

Stan had a goal too. His goal was to have a well-run Pathfinder club and to keep his charges happy. But can older teenagers discipline and effectively manage younger teenagers? Well, you might conclude that it could be a recipe for disaster, and, generally speaking, that is probably true. Read Stan's story and see how he coped when he was caught in that very uncomfortable scenario.

*****

Stan was a nineteen-year-old counselor for a Pathfinder Club in southern California. The young group he was to oversee was an energetic, friendly, curious group of teenage boys with one exception: Brad. Brad was a bully. He was such a bully that he was making life miserable for the other teens in Stan's group. Brad's bullying consisted mainly of name calling, but his words stung like fire, and the guys were complaining. Camp, one of the highlights of the summer, was turning out to be a nightmare for Stan's charges.

What to do? Stan prayed about the situation, and the Holy Spirit impressed him to talk with Brad. Perhaps he could reason with this young bully and stop the name-calling. Finding an occasion to talk to Brad, Stan asked, "Do you realize you're hurting the guys' feelings by calling such terrible names?"

"Aw, it's nothing," Brad responded.

"But you're hurting their feelings," Stan could see he was getting nowhere with this young man.

> *Would it hurt your feelings if I called you nasty names?*

"Would it hurt your feelings if I called you nasty names?" Stan thought he would turn the oppressor into the oppressed.

"Of course not. I wouldn't be hurt," the bully answered confidently. So, with a mission in mind, Stan waited for an appropriate opportunity to test the truth of Brad's statement. And the opportunity came.

"Hey, you _____," Stan called across the dorm room. Brad winced, but Stan wouldn't give up. After landing a few more unsavory titles on the bully, Stan talked with Brad.

"Did that hurt your feelings?" He watched Brad's face closely.

"Yes," Brad admitted. "It did."

"Well," Stan replied, "I didn't mean what I said to you, but I wanted you to know how it feels when you are the recipient of nasty names."

Ten years later, Stan approached the market's cashier and waited in line for his turn.

"Hello, Mr. Jackson." The young cashier gave him a friendly greeting. "Do you remember me?"

"I'm sorry, but I'm afraid I don't remember you." Stan had an apologetic tone in his voice.

"I'm Brad. I'm the bully who you talked to long ago. What you did that day changed my life."

Stan instantly remembered the whole scenario: the unhappy group of boys, the mouthy bully, his prayer asking the Lord what he should do, the answer, and now here in front of him was a transformed young man! What a blessing. God is so good to care enough to take the time to help a young camp counselor find a solution and to help a young man change an awful mouthy habit!

CHAPTER 15

THE INTERPRETER

The second chapter in the book of Acts tells of the Holy Spirit descending on the Lord's disciples. As they told the story of salvation, they spoke in at least sixteen different languages so those who came from afar to Jerusalem could understand the salvation story and could then transmit this fabulous story to their kinsfolk. The Holy Spirit works in similar ways today. Samuel has a story to tell which will convince you that this is, indeed, true.

*****

Twenty-three-year-old Samuel carefully prepared the sermons for his upcoming evangelistic meetings. He was to be speaking in Gridley, California. When he arrived, he found that the congregation had several Spanish-speaking attendees included in the English-speaking church. The meetings always started with prayer, asking for the Lord's presence and with the desire that the people's minds would be open to accept the end-time messages that would be presented. Samuel and the more mature pastors knew the vital truths presented to this congregation needed to be understood and appreciated by the people. It was a matter of being ready for the Second Coming and they realized the seriousness of their roles as leaders and pastors to this precious flock.

One of the women who attended the meetings had not yet learned English, so it was a curiosity to Samuel why she even came. Obviously, it must not have been very interesting for her to sit through the meetings, but he was happy for this lovely lady to come even if they could not communicate.

At the end of the series, one of the woman's family members confided in Samuel that this lady wanted to ask Samuel some questions about what was presented.

"Questions?" Samuel's attention was caught. "If she cannot understand what I have spoken this evening, how can she have questions?"

"Oh, but she did understand you. She understood every word you spoke, and she wants to know more."

This experience reminds us of John 16:13. "Howbeit when he, the Spirit of truth, is come, he will guide you into all truth…." The Holy Spirit was present at the meeting that night because He had been invited, and in spite of the language differences, every word was understood, and more questions needed to be answered. It does remind us of Pentecost, doesn't it?

CHAPTER 16

EVEN THE WIND AND THE RAIN OBEY HIM

Luke 8:22–25 tells an amazing story of Jesus' power over even the elements. Here's how Luke describes the scene:

Now it came to pass on a certain day, that he went into a ship with his disciples: and he said unto them, Let us go over unto the other side of the lake. And they launched forth. But as they sailed he fell asleep: and there came down a storm of wind on the lake; and they were filled with water, and were in jeopardy. And they came to him, and awoke him, saying, Master, master, we perish. Then he arose, and rebuked the wind and the raging of the water: and they ceased, and there was a calm. And he said unto them, Where is your faith? And they being afraid wondered, saying one to another, What manner of man is this! for he commandeth even the winds and water, and they obey him.

The disciples experienced this miracle 2,000 years ago, but is this generation able to observe the same kinds of miracles? Read the next story and then decide.

*****

Brock Smith folded the papers on his desk after the Pathfinder meeting. As deputy director of the club, he felt a sense of satisfaction leading this group of twelve to fifteen-year-olds in the early 1970s. Corralling some of their boisterous energy and answering their endless questions gave him a genuine purpose in life, and he enjoyed his job.

"Mr. Smith?" Brock looked up to see young Jeremy standing in front of the desk.

"Yes, Jeremy. How can I help you?" Brock noticed a look of sadness in Jeremy's eyes.

"Mr. Smith, when can we go camping again? I love to go camping! We haven't gone for a long time."

Brock gave a deep sigh. "Yes, Jeremy, I know, I know. We've had to cancel camping trips several times due to many factors. I'll tell you what. I'll talk with the director of the club and see if we somehow can plan a camping trip soon."

"Yeah!" Jeremy's face lit up. "Please do talk with him. All the boys want to go on a camping trip."

Shortly thereafter, Brock called Tom Lampson, the director of the club.

"Tom, we're going to have to plan a camping trip for our young charges. Jeremy talked with me and told me how much our group wants a trip. You know what this means to the boys socially, and it's a good physical and mental workout for them, too. Most of all, so many of our boys are impacted spiritually as they listen to the talks around the campfire. Do you suppose we can plan a trip for them soon?"

Tom's response was slow. "You know, Brock, I've been thinking about this for a while, too. Winter is not exactly the right time of year for a backpacking trip, but we've put this off far too long. Let me look at my calendar, and we'll put something together in the next couple of weeks."

The excitement built when the thirty boys learned they were to prepare for a backpacking trip to Joshua Tree National Monument. What fun! That area had been chosen because it was a fairly level hike to the camping site, which was perfect for the younger backpacking boys. Two trusted teenage counselors would also be joining the group.

On the day appointed, with great anticipation, everyone assembled in the church's parking lot, loaded their gear, said goodbye to parents, and drove off to a weekend of great adventure. However, unbeknownst to them, much more than fun was in store for them this weekend. They would see God's hand at work.

When they arrived at the camp, several looked up at the sky with consternation. "Oh no!" Tom said. "Look at the rain! How can we have a good time if we're wet all weekend?" Tom looked at Brock. "Do you suppose we should cancel this trip? It's going to be a miserable weekend with thirty kids sitting in their tents all day long."

"I don't know," Brock said. "Why don't we pray about it and ask the Lord if we should set up tents or if we should go home?"

"Good idea. Let's pray."

The entire group bowed their heads and asked God what they should do. After praying, they felt impressed that they should go ahead and set up their tents. From the moment the tents were set, the rain stopped. That weekend was memorable as they hiked, ate wonderful food, worshipped, sang together, and told unforgettable stories around the campfire. Not one drop of rain or snow fell on the camping group the entire weekend. In fact, there was not even a cloud in the sky. However, when it was time to go home, and the tents were loaded in the cars, the rain began to fall.

When they arrived home, they found that it had rained and snowed one hundred miles in every direction around them all weekend long, yet a circle of clear weather had covered their tents. Everyone was struck by the fact that our Father in heaven managed the weather so that the Pathfinder club could have the benefit of a memorable weekend.

CHAPTER 17

GOD'S GENEROUS HAND

Malachi 3:8–10 issues a command accompanied by a promise.

> Will a man rob God? Yet ye have robbed me. But ye say, Wherein have we robbed thee? In tithes and offerings. Ye are cursed with a curse: for ye have robbed me, even this whole nation. Bring ye all the tithes into the storehouse, that there may be meat in mine house, and prove me now herewith, saith the LORD of hosts, if I will not open you the windows of heaven, and pour you out a blessing, that there shall not be room enough to receive it.

Through the years, this command has been challenging to many, especially to those whose income is limited. Florin was one such person who struggled with the idea of giving one-tenth of his small income to the Lord. You will find his story encouraging and another proof that God's Word is sure.

*****

Florin was a hard-working young man with a wife and two daughters to support. Life was not easy in communist Romania. He worked long hours, and, even then, their life was not even close to a life of luxury. In fact, just to acquire the basics for living was very difficult.

Florin's wife had been baptized into the Seventh-day Adventist Church, and he felt drawn to the truths she had learned there. Over the years Florin had become a close friend of the pastor of the church, Pastor Bagdu. As they talked, the pastor explained the biblical doctrines that their church followed, which included tithing.

Florin wanted to join his wife as a member of the Seventh-day Adventist Church, but he was an honest man, and he knew that he could not accept the tithing principle. Life was so hard as it was and to take ten percent of his income and give it to the church? Impossible! So he refused to be baptized because he knew he could not honestly accept all the church taught.

One day, Pastor Bagdu met with Florin, and the tithe subject came up again. "Why don't you try tithing for one month?" the pastor asked. "God has told you to test Him, so just do it and see what happens." Florin looked carefully at his special friend. Could it be that the pastor was right? Okay, for one month he would test God and see if those promised blessings would come flooding in.

> *At the end of the month after paying tithe, he had more money than in previous months.*

During that next month, amazing things began to happen. Florin's boss asked him if he would be willing to put in overtime hours, so many hours were added to his paycheck. Then the bills started coming in, but Florin noticed they were not as high as before. They were decreased! In fact, at the end of the month after paying tithe, he had more money than in previous months. He was convinced and was baptized, and he continued to be blessed as he was faithful to God. Florin was a man with limited education, but because he was now so financially blessed, he could help others who needed financial assistance.

People would ask, "How do you have all of this?"

Florin would answer, "You cannot out-give God. The more we give Him, the more He blesses." God's hand was over Florin's finances honoring Florin's faith and action.

CHAPTER 18

JESUS LOVES THE LITTLE CHILDREN

Jesus know the needs of children, and He loves to listen to their prayers. Let the children shut out the world and everything that would attract the thoughts from God; and let them feel that they are alone with God, that His eye looks into the inmost heart and reads the desire of the soul, and that they may talk with God…. (*The Adventist Home*, p. 299)

Walter learned to talk with God as a very young child, and he had an earnest desire to live in heaven someday. His life story reveals God's protective hand multiple times during Walter's growing up and young adult years. Walter believes his heart search for God during his childhood made the difference in the outcome of his life. You will enjoy reading his story.

*****

The heavy gate squeakily swung open as three-year-old Walter pushed against it with all his might. Young Walter was often left to entertain himself while his busy family attended to chores on their farm. Now, being bored with life on the inside of the fence, Walter wondered what lay outside the gate. Soon his baby feet were hurrying down the road faster and faster until, before long, he had traveled about half a mile. Then, he heard a most intriguing sound—the sound of rushing water. Excitedly, he peered at one of the dikes next to the river that had been built to slow the water down. As he leaned in farther and farther to play with the water, he soon found himself completely immersed and then coming to the surface gasping for breath. Now, the struggle for survival began. Over and over, his tiny hands tried to claw his way up the sides of the dike, but he fell back again over and over. With water-logged clothes and decreasing energy, the hope of his getting to the top of the dike was fading. Finally, he was able to hang on tenaciously and made it to the top of the dike. When he arrived home three and a half hours later, his frantic family came running to meet him. After much fruitless searching, they were tearfully relieved to see him walking up the driveway!

Perhaps it was his mother's prayers or even young Walter's prayers that preserved him that day in the dike. For in spite of her very busy schedule, Walter's mother read the Bible to him very often and taught him how to pray. The book of Revelation and its description of heaven especially intrigued him. As he walked through the dark woods at night and gazed at the stars, Walter knew there was a God in heaven and other worlds were out there. How much he desired to go to heaven! He thought many times about Jesus and knew that He was the Person to go to if there was trouble.

However, Walter wasn't always sure he would make it to heaven and worried that he would be left out of that wonderful place. Perhaps to allay his fears, his mother taught him a prayer of contrition. Over and over, Walter would ask God to forgive him for his sins because he felt sure he would be lost. How much he wanted to go to heaven! Certainly God heard those prayers as Walter's life proved later.

At age six, Walter and his sister, Joanie, had the job of bringing the cows home in the dark. Listening for the cows' bells, they called, "Here, Boss!" Upon finding the cows, Walter would hold the cow's tail, and Joanie would hang onto Walter. It was so dark that they couldn't see, but the cows knew the way home.

One night, Walter and Joanie walked past a small cabin near their home when, looking further up the hill, they stared at a huge, gray timber wolf about forty feet away. "Run, Joanie, run! Walter yelled as they ran through the thick snow back to the cabin. Their wild pounding on the door aroused the cabin's owner, who grabbed a gun once he heard their story. Between the wolves and the bears (his sister once counted thirty-three bears in a clover field), it was a wild country they lived in, but God's hand was over them every day.

Walter always felt comfortable around the farm's animals until a large Angus bull tore down part of the fence and charged Walter and the herd of cows he was near. A large heifer saw the bull coming and began running towards the creek. Walter ran as hard and as fast as the cows and when they reached the creek, he simply hung on to the last cow's tail and skipped across the creek to safety.

Age nine was a particularly eventful year for this young man. When his parents were gone, his oldest brother would wrap a rope around a steer's neck, sit on the steer, and go bucking out the narrow barn door until the steer dumped him off. Of course, each brother had to have a turn, and even young Walter would take the violent ride on the great steer. Looking back, Walter realizes how dangerous this "fun" play was and thanks God that he was not seriously hurt or killed.

However, one day he was hurt. As he was walking on the second floor of the barn, he fell through, landed a story below on a manger, and broke his arm. Unfortunately, that wasn't the end of this nine-year-old's excitement. Sometime later, he and his siblings were out sledding. After the older children were bored with that activity, they left young Walter to find his way home alone. He followed the barbed wire fence back to the house. As he walked, he noticed he was more tired than usual. Then he looked down and saw blood gushing out of his wrist. Apparently, he had seriously cut his wrist on the barbed wire. By the time he arrived home the front of his clothes were bloody, and he had lost so much blood that he was unusually weak. His mother rushed him to the hospital for stiches.

Later, Walter lived in an orphanage for two years because his mother became ill, but he had a sense of God's presence during those difficult years. Here he was separated from all but one of his siblings. Without parental advice, it was a challenge to know how to best adjust to the demands of the workers at the orphanage. But he worked hard milking cows there, and even though the orphanage didn't provide much formal education for him, Walter learned how to get along with almost everyone.

When we look at the next years of Walter's life, it appears that all his life-long prayers offered him unusual protection. Such as when he was in the Navy and his ship, the USS Borie, had left Norfolk, Virginia, for a refueling exercise. The sea was a little choppy but calmed down when the Borie came alongside on the starboard side to connect with the fuel hose of a tanker. Walter and his division were to pull the tanker's lines over to the Borie. Walter's position was at the end of the rope, and he was coiling it on the Borie's deck.

Suddenly, Walter heard an incredibly loud noise, and, looking up, he saw a rogue wave crashing over their ship. He described it as sounding like a freight train. The only thing he could grab on to was a boat winch in front of him. As the wave hit, he was instantly pulled away from the winch and tossed into the wave. The wave threw him so his rib cage was slammed against the chain link railing. After the wave subsided, he felt himself being swept along the deck, sliding under the chain link. Quickly, he grabbed the chain link and was able to stay on the deck. However, his legs and hips were caught in the rope he had just coiled. He could feel it tightening around his hips and legs and knew that the rope could get caught in the ship's screws which meant he would be pulled into the ocean. He was finally able to kick free from the rope and was not seriously hurt. Several of his crew members were injured, and there were six ambulances awaiting the ship's arrival at the pier when they returned to Norfolk.

There was another time when his ship was in the North Atlantic, and the collision alarm began to sound. Walter was in the hanger bay when he heard the alarm and looked up to see a large oil tanker headed towards the Bowie. The Bowie reduced her engines but was hit on the port side in the bow. Walter explained that the collision was so great it almost knocked him down. The anchor of the Bowie made an eighteen-foot gash in the bow of the tanker. If the gash had been another eight feet long, the anchor would have ripped into the fuel tank of the tanker. Walter realized the ending of that event would have been much different if the fuel tank had been opened by the anchor.

Part of Walter's job was to retrieve exercise torpedoes. Once, when he was in the water, he heard gun shots, and, looking towards the ship, he saw several gunner's mates shooting his direction. Later, when he was once again on board the ship, these men said they thought sharks were circling around him. Walter had not seen the sharks, and this experience made him nervous about retrieving torpedoes in the future. But since he was the lead torpedo man on the USS Borie, he was required to swim out to the exercise torpedo and wait there until the ship came to retrieve him and the torpedo.

One day, an exercise torpedo was shot while the ocean was very rough with huge waves. Walter put his life vest on and then attached a pull line to his belt loop. This was necessary since he would swim fifty to seventy-five yards away from the ship to retrieve the torpedo. Once Walter was in the water, he could not see the torpedo, so he followed the hand signals of the officer on deck. However, the ship was not traveling farther away, so Walter took off the haul line and continued to try to follow the hand signals of the officer.

Now the sea became even rougher, and he could not see the ship except for smoke from its smokestacks. Walter knew that if the torpedo was silent, sonar would not locate him. He had now drifted far apart from the ship, and he realized the ship would have to come looking for him, which would be like looking for a needle in a haystack. Also, Walter tried to keep his eye on the torpedo since it sank deeply in the ocean with the swells and then abruptly would rise to the surface. He feared he would be injured by it hitting him and, also, that it might sink.

After about an hour of being in the water, it was increasingly difficult for Walter to stay close to the torpedo, which was sinking deeper and deeper, and the ocean swells were rolling over him. Suddenly, he looked up, and there was the Borie next to him. The sailors threw the strap down to wrap around the torpedo, and then Walter tried to climb the rope ladder up the ship's side. The water was around seventy degrees, but the air was much colder, and, try as he might, Walter was too exhausted to get his foot on the bottom rung of the rope ladder. His hands were very cold, so he slipped back into the water to warm up. Over and over he tried to climb the ladder. Finally, he was able to slowly climb the ladder up to the deck. Someone put a blanket around him and helped him to his bunk. He knew he had nearly been lost at sea, and it was a miracle the ship was able to find him in that vast ocean.

And then there were the head injuries. One happened when he slipped on steps going to a lower level of the ship. He hit his head on a torpedo, which almost knocked him out. When he tried to get up, his head was spinning, and he could not walk. His crewmates carried him to the ship's infirmary where he rested for three days. Still, he was ill for two weeks and suffered from several headaches after this injury.

Another head injury occurred while Walter was in a gun mount. He realized that one of the guns had not fired as the other guns were firing, so he decided to crawl out of the gun mount to investigate when the gun suddenly fired. One of the projectiles that was bolted over the door had come loose due to the vibration and fell on Walter's head, shoulder, and lower back. When the gun crew returned, they found Walter half hanging out of the exit hatch. He spent time in the infirmary and has ringing in his ears to this day. These kinds of experiences gave Walter terrible dreams after he came home from the Navy. He would awaken to find his mother standing by his bedside. He wondered why she was there, and she would explain that she had come because he had been screaming with all his might.

How can one man escape all these near-death experiences and live to tell the story? Those early sessions with his mother reading the Bible to him laid the foundation of his thinking. Walter is now a committed Bible student and believes that those early childhood prayers offered from a sincere, honest heart as well as his sincere desire to go to heaven had much to do with preserving his life these seventy-eight years.

One outstanding author has put it this way:

> I saw that every prayer which is sent up in faith from an honest heart, will be heard of God and answered; and the one that sent up the petition will have the blessing when he needs it most, and it will often exceed his expectations. Not a prayer of a true saint is lost if sent up in faith from an honest heart. (*Gospel Workers*, 1892/1893 ed., p. 114)

Walter, your prayers were answered. And, yes, if you are faithful to our Father in heaven, your childhood desire to go to heaven someday will be realized.

CHAPTER 19

THE POWER OF PRAYER

Prayers, whether spoken quickly or while we are meditating, can have an incredible effect on our everyday lives. It is very important to spend time with God in the morning, laying our plans at His feet and committing our way to Him. The following stories demonstrate the value of carefully praying on a daily basis as well as being ready to offer prayers for guidance, health, loved ones, and safety all through the day.

*****

Jonathon and his wife bought a car with problems that had over 200,000 miles on its odometer. It was all they could afford at that time. The car was needed to get Jonathon to his window-cleaning jobs while he was enrolled in graduate school. Unfortunately, at times, the car would simply stop and refuse to move.

Yikes, Jonathon thought after arriving at one of his jobs. *I'm stranded, and I need to get to my next assignment.* He would look under the hood and try to estimate what the issues were, but he knew this car needed lots of help, and since he was new to the area, he didn't even know who to ask for help. He certainly could not afford to take it to a garage for mechanical repairs. So, having had much experience in going to the Lord, Jonathon would pray for the car to start. And it started. Again and again, this scenario was repeated.

Jonathon even drove the unpredictable car from Michigan to Florida, and they made it back home. For two and a half years, the troublesome car continued to start after prayer was offered. When Jonathon was hired to be an associate pastor, the infamous car refused to start. Now Jonathon could afford to hire a mechanic to remedy this car's ills, and the miracle was no longer needed.

One author has put it this way:

> There is no time or place in which it is inappropriate to offer up a petition to God. There is nothing that can prevent us from lifting up our hearts in the spirit of earnest prayer. In the crowds of the street, in the midst of a business engagement, we may send up a petition to God and plead for divine guidance, as did Nehemiah when he made his request before King Artaxerxes. A closet of communion may be found wherever we are. We should have the door of the heart open continually and our invitation going up that Jesus may come and abide as a heavenly guest in the soul. (*Steps to Christ*, p. 99)

Maybe there are advantages to having little money and a broken-down car. It's when we are helpless that we realize our great need for God's assistance in times of need. The poor man leaning on the Lord is, in reality, much richer than the wealthy man who ignores Him. Jonathon certainly learned that God is our Helper, even for a car that refused to start.

*****

Sometimes a prayer must be spoken in a second or two. Nigel found our Father in heaven even answers these kinds of prayers.

*****

Nigel settled back in his car seat and hit the gas. Life was good. He had a free weekend, and he had a date with the very attractive Suzie. Thoughts of Suzie ran through his mind as he raced along the country road.

Suddenly, Nigel saw a ninety degree turn in the road, and a telephone pole in front of the car. "God, help me!" he yelled. Whizzing past the telephone pole, his car came to a stop in a vineyard. Again, he prayed, "God, please help me get out of here." Starting the car, he drove between the grape vines and back onto the road. Once again on his way, Nigel paid close attention to his driving and didn't indulge in any more daydreaming about Suzie. From a grateful heart he prayed, "Thank you, dear God, for saving me from hitting the telephone pole and for getting me out of the vineyard. I just experienced a miracle! My weekend would have been much different if You had not helped me! Thank you, thank you."

*****

Have you ever been saved from having to pay a huge sum of money? That's exactly what happened to a group of hikers who were at Pine Springs Ranch for a relaxed weekend. See how prayer kept them from a having to pay a huge fee.

*****

"Hey! Why don't you join us for a hike? They say this trail is a loop and will only take an hour or two to get back here." Charlotte heard her two brothers call to one of the girls in the group.

"Mary and I will follow you three in just a few minutes!" Charlotte yelled.

The young adults retreat at Pine Springs Ranch had proved to be a real blessing to all who attended, and now, on Sabbath afternoon, the autumn weather seemed to be calling for a brisk walk in the woods. Soon Charlotte and Mary began up the trail, which they noticed was not well-traveled and quite narrow. After hiking for several minutes, they came to a fork in the trail and could hear the three hikers ahead of them. It became apparent that this trail was not a loop, so Charlotte and Mary decided to turn around and follow the path down the hill. Yelling to her brothers, Charlotte called, "Turn around. This trail is not a loop! We're going back down the trail."

As Charlotte and Mary descended the trail, they came to the fork in the path. Which path to follow? After turning to the left and walking for several minutes, Charlotte realized they were on the wrong path, so they retraced their steps to the fork in the road.

When they arrived at the camp, Charlotte began looking for her brothers' group. No one had seen them. It was now dark, and the group began to call loudly for the lost hikers. The group also began to pray. More time went by, and someone decided to call the ranger station to see if they could help. Two rangers arrived and asked Charlotte what the hikers were wearing and what were they carrying. "They were wearing jeans and light shirts. I think they also had water with them. No. No one was carrying a jacket," Charlotte's voice was now concerned because three hours has passed at this point. Although she knew they would not freeze to death at night in this fall weather, she also knew it would be a very uncomfortable, cold night for them out on the trail.

The two rangers combed the trails without finding the hikers and decided to call for a helicopter search team. The helicopters circled around and around the mountain for two hours but without success. Their low altitude created quite a racket, which caused two monks who lived in a monastery on the mountain to walk down to Pine Springs Ranch.

"What's the problem?" they asked.

"Three people are lost on the trail," Charlotte told them. "That's the reason for the helicopters. We're praying they'll be found since it's a cold night." Prayers were now earnestly ascending from individuals and small groups that had gathered together.

The two monks disappeared, but within half an hour, they returned with the three lost hikers. The monks knew this mountain's trails very well and were able to quickly locate the hikers. "Praise the Lord!" shouts of praises were given to God, and many thanks were given to the monks.

Later, Charlotte and her brothers learned that if the helicopter crew had found them, they would have been charged $160,000. Our Father in heaven heard the prayers of many young adults and saved three hikers from a very uncomfortable night on the trail and much money by helping them to be found before the helicopter crew spotted them. He had intervened once again!

****

Lois is well aware of the importance of morning prayer because of an experience that could have been fatal. Here is her story:

*****

Lois ended her morning prayer with, "And Lord, please be with me and my family today. Amen." It had been Lois' habit for many years to have a morning worship time before starting her day. Life had taught her that it was precarious to begin the day without prayer and Bible study. Unexpected surprises and challenges had a way of showing up throughout her lifetime, but she knew Jesus, her personal Friend, could manage any situation. Therefore, the habit of prayer first thing in the morning had been established in her daily routine.

Okay, Lois thought as she rose from her knees. *What needs to be done today? Well, it's very hot outside so for sure the front lawn and the rose bushes need to be watered. Oh yes, the trees in the back need to be fertilized, too.* The thought of fertilizing the trees behind the house made Lois pause. Those trees had been planted on a seventy-degree angle on the hillside. From the bottom of the hill, it almost appeared to be straight up, and the hill ended in a concrete ditch at the bottom of twenty feet. *Oh well,* Lois reassured herself. *I've fertilized those trees many times before, and as long as I take my big stick for balance, I'll be fine.*

Going to the garage to find the large walking stick, Lois remembered to make sure the stick was solidly in the ground in order to provide support for her on the hillside. Finding the stick and the fertilizer, Lois began the steep climb to the first tree at the top of the hill. With the stick solidly in the ground as an anchor to keep her balance, Lois patiently filled the mulched area around the tree with fertilizer. Proceeding to the second tree, Lois felt herself slipping as the walking stick suddenly lost its hold in the ground. Falling to the ground, Lois began to roll downward. Faster and faster, she rolled until, in just a matter of seconds, she covered the twenty feet to the bottom of the hill. Hitting the concrete culvert with a thud, Lois lay there for several seconds finding it difficult to breathe. After regaining a sense of where she was, Lois wondered if any of her bones were broken. Cautiously moving her limbs, she realized she was not seriously injured. Carefully getting up, Lois found that there was only a small scratch on her knee. "Surely, my angel was with me today!" she exclaimed.

Lois recounted what she had just experienced and realized she could have been killed or broken her neck or had serious head injuries or broken bones—but there was no evidence of any serious injury at all. "Thank you, Lord, for watching over me today," she exclaimed with heartfelt thanks. "I did not see my guardian angel, but I have strong evidence that angelic protection was given to me today. You have answered my morning prayer. Thank you, Lord! Praise Your holy name!"

*****

This next story illustrates how a vacation can turn into an unpleasant time unless God is our Helper. Bob and Shelley nearly turned around to go back home. Frustration was building!

*****

"What's wrong with this crazy clam shell? We've had a new ball put on this trailer, and I can't get the clam shell off!" Bob was exasperated as he attempted to remove the cover over the ball on the trailer.

"Here, let me help you." Shelley, Bob's wife, stepped closer to him. "Between the two of us, we should be able to get that cover off."

The two of them pulled over and over, even lifting the trailer up in the process, but without success. Twenty minutes of struggling with the cover had tired them both. What they did not realize was that rain had caused the metals to rust and fuse together.

"Let's go into the trailer and pray," Shelley suggested. Willing to take a break, Bob followed his wife into the trailer. "Dear God," Shelley said, "You know we need to remove the clam shell to unhitch the trailer from the pick-up. We've tried and tried and can't get it off. Please help us." With that, Bob and Shelley returned to the front of the trailer to remove the clam shell. In one minute, the clam shell pulled up, and the hook could be lifted off the ball of the trailer.

"Thank you, Lord!"

Bob and Shelley were earnest Christians who had started this trip with a prayer for safety and that God would be with them. However, it was a trip that produced several challenges to the point that Shelley asked, "Bob, do you think we're supposed to make this trip? It seems like every time we turn around there's a problem. Maybe we should just go home." But, after some discussion, they decided to continue their vacation travels.

At one point, when Shelley was driving through Las Vegas, she missed the turn-off to their destination: Verdi, Nevada. Not being a seasoned driver of a pick-up pulling a trailer, Shelley concluded she would take the next exit and turn around in a large truck-stop parking area to get her bearings, so she could decide what to do next. In the parking lot was a young man sitting in a tow truck.

"Can you help me? I missed the turnoff to Verdi, and I don't know which way to go now." Shelley's voice had a pleading tone.

"Just go to 580 north, and it will take you to the Verdi turnoff," he had a confident ring in his response.

"How do I get to 580 north?"

"It's right there." The tow truck driver pointed to the highway entrance a short distance away.

"Thank you so much. You've been very helpful." Shelley felt great relief to be put back on course towards Verdi.

Soon Shelley and Bob were on their way, and the route they now took was even easier than if Shelley had taken the first exit. They're trip was enjoyable, even if stressful at times, and they arrived home safely, thanking God for His help in all the details of their lives. Yes, they realized when looking back over this enjoyable/stressful vacation, He is willing to help even with small problems.

CHAPTER 20

ANGELS AROUND US

One of the reasons I have taken the time to collect these stories is because my school children loved to hear angel stories. We even reread an angel book. And I thought, *Wait a minute! God's hand is still at work today as much as in the past. There must be thousands of angel stories out there that need to be told.*

Here are a few angel stories that remind us how close the unseen world is to our world. Read Marcie's story and see if it doesn't send chills down your back. Her story will be an encouragement to you to know that divine intervention is nearer than we usually realize.

*****

Marcie carefully lifted herself into the cab of the large truck and surveyed her situation. The truck belonged to her brother-in-law's mother who needed it transported north. Marcie had been told to make sure the gas tank did not fall below the quarter tank level, or she would have difficulty filling it. Marcie knew she would soon be traveling several hours from Central California to home in Northern California since it was her nephew, Jerry's, birthday, and she had been given permission to take a few days off from the colporteur team to be with her family for the celebration.

It had been hot, hard work selling religious and health books from door-to-door during the heat-filled summer months, but it was a way to pay for her college education. And the work had been rewarding. Realizing her family would be interested in seeing the books she was selling, she gathered several and threw them on the truck seat.

The first couple of hours were uneventful as Marcie drove up Interstate 5. As she neared the town of Goshen, however, she looked down at the gas gauge and realized she needed to get gas, so she reached for her purse on the passenger's side. After flipping it open and looking for money, she realized she didn't have money because she had loaned it to a friend, and the friend had not yet paid it back.

Panic began to creep into Marcie's mind. She knew she didn't have credit cards, and she was hours from home and soon to run out of gas. Then, she remembered the books. Of course! She would simply sell those books door to door. Dark clouds lined the horizon, and she realized it was nearing sunset and not an ideal time to be knocking on doors, but it was the only answer to a nearly desperate situation.

Taking exit 98A into Goshen, she came to a new housing development where only a few new homes were built. Putting her head on the steering wheel, Marcie prayed, "Dear God, help me. I need your help. It's almost dark, and I'm stranded here. Please, please help me." Marcie will tell the rest of the story:

> I picked up all the books and pamphlets and cautiously slid out of the truck. Walking up to the first house, I rang the doorbell, and a woman opened the door. I explained to her that I was a college student working my way through school by selling books and then gave her the canvas I had learned so well that summer. Surveying all the material, she decided to give me twenty-five cents for a small pamphlet.
>
> Disappointed but striving to keep my courage up, I reminded myself that this kind of work required persistence, so I kept walking up the

street to the next home. The garage door was open, and a police car was in the driveway. Since I didn't have a permit to work this area, I decided to keep walking, but a man called to me from the garage, "What are you doing?"

Again, I explained the work I was doing and why. I attempted to tell him about the books, but he stopped me and said, "Let me see your books." Then after a brief look, he said, "Stay here for a minute." Soon he returned, handed me a one-hundred-dollar bill, and said, "I'll take all of those books. I have relatives that can use them." I stared in disbelief. I explained to him that I would never charge this much for the books, but he insisted that I keep the one hundred dollars.

The whole transaction had not taken more than five minutes. Thanking him profusely, I returned to the truck, closed the door, put my head on the steering wheel, and sobbed my thanks to our heavenly Father for his protection and answer to my prayer for help. Soon, I filled the gas tank and was on my way home to tell my family of God's merciful answer to my prayer.

Sometime later, I followed the same road, knowing exactly where I had turned off. Goshen, exit 91. But I COULD NOT FIND THE NEW HOMES. Traveling around several blocks, I looked and looked for the homes where the miracle had occurred, but I could never find them! Could it be that our Father in heaven had created new homes with angels answering the doors just for my benefit? Someday, it will all be explained to me. God is great, God is good. Praise His name!

*****

Colporteurs are special people. They endure cold, heat, doors slammed in their faces, arguments, and discouragement, as they seek to place God's word in people's homes. Marcie's story was phenomenal, and Terry, as a colporteur, also had indications that an angel was accompanying him as he knocked on doors. Here's his story:

*****

It was the summer of 2012, and young Terry was in a small, farming community near Bakersfield, California. This summer he was colporteuring (selling religious books) door-to-door. It had been a long day, and now it was pitch black and after 9:00 in the evening.

Terry was knocking on doors by himself when he came to a door that he believes was a divine appointment. A man opened the door who had once been a Seventh-day Adventist. In the course of their conversation, Terry explained his church affiliation, and the two had a very good, in-depth discussion about spiritual topics.

At last, the owner of the house said, "Let me get you some water," and he left Terry at the door. Soon he returned with two bottles of water.

"Here," he said. "Here's a bottle for you and a bottle for your buddy."

My buddy? thought Terry. *Who's he talking about?*

Terry thought maybe another colporteur had come up behind him, and he looked around. No one was there. Besides, it was very dark outside, and one could not easily see even if someone else were there. As Terry thought about this later, he wondered if this gentleman had been allowed to see Terry's guardian angel, for he remembered the following quotation:

> Every canvasser has positive and constant need of the angelic ministration; for he has an important work to do, a work that he cannot do in his own strength. Those who are born again, who are willing to be guided by the Holy Spirit, doing in Christ's way that which they can do, those who will work as if they could see the heavenly universe watching them, will be accompanied and instructed by holy angels, who will go before them to the dwellings of the people, preparing the way for them. (*Testimonies for the Church*, vol. 6, p. 319)

*****

Samuel was another colporteur who believes angels went before him when he learned to pray during one summer in Utah. The turn-around in sales was not happenstance. Samuel knows that for sure.

*****

Seventeen-year-old Samuel lay outside looking at the stars. How discouraging life looked! Here was a shy, timid, scared young man going door-to-door in Salt Lake City, Utah, and having no success at all.

As a colporteur his goal was to get as many of the big message books into the homes of the people, and for five weeks of this summer, he had only been able to get people to buy small pamphlets and books. Just enough to pay for his gas every day. To top it all, circumstances had been arranged so that he had not been trained to sell the big books nor had he sold the paperback magabooks first, as other colporteurs had done.

He knew when he started colporteuring here that it would be a challenge since most people living in the area belonged to a different church. But even those who were not of that fellowship didn't want the books he was selling. It was so overwhelming! Samuel was tempted to think that God was not listening to him as he prayed for success.

And so, under the stars night after night, Samuel truly learned to pray. In fact, he had never prayed this way before as he struggled with God. And those earnest prayers paid off! Suddenly, people began to buy the big books. In fact, his sales increased on a daily basis, and he knew God had answered his prayers by preparing the minds of the people to buy the big books before he knocked on their doors.

Colporteuring that summer stretched Samuel. It forced him to confront his fears and to confirm his relationship with God, but a discouraging summer turned into a memorable experience in which Samuel learned the value of earnest prayer.

CHAPTER 21

HELPERS IN TIMES OF NEED

Sometimes angels just show up, leaving us amazed that they can appear and disappear at will. Sue had this kind of experience. The man didn't enter the room through the door or a window, yet he was in the room. The story of this man's presence has been told and retold in one family because of the role he played in their mother's recovery from illness. Here is what happened:

*****

Sue was a young woman in her mid-thirties. She had a long history of illness and now she had extreme nasal issues, which caused severe breathing difficulties. One day, as she fought to get her next breath, she called her son, Jason, and told him to run to the neighbor, Mrs. Henley, to get help. Recognizing the seriousness of the situation, Jason ran two doors to Mrs. Henley's house and blurted out his mother's cry for aid. The neighbor quickly came and used measures to help Sue breathe more easily.

Eventually, Sue was hospitalized, and as she lay on the hospital bed, she thought about how the doctors stated she had gangrene in her sinuses (this was the day before penicillin or other antibiotics). As she mulled all of this over, she became very, very discouraged. Her situation seemed extremely bleak to her since she had three young children to raise and was totally incapable of even getting out of bed, let alone having the ability to take care of young children.

Then Sue turned her thoughts to God. In her distress, she asked the Lord to give her some indication that He was still with her. Suddenly, a very well-dressed, kind-looking man appeared at the foot of her bed and quietly stood there. Although he said nothing, his presence was very, very comforting, and peace flooded over Sue. She felt a calmness, and Sue knew that God was with her. While she continued looking at her Visitor, He disappeared. To the end of her long life, Sue believed that a divine Presence came to her that day in answer to her desperate prayer for assurance of God's presence. Sue eventually became well and was able to raise her children and to enjoy her grandchildren.

*****

Sometimes, angels will allow themselves to be seen. Such was the case when a group of over thirty people needed help. The angels' disappearance kept the group searching.

*****

In the early 1970s, the San Bernardino Pathfinder Club had about thirty members. In addition, they had included sixteen to eighteen-year-old junior counselors who were very dependable and trustworthy. Since these youngsters had unlimited energy, it was decided to take them for a long hike at the Joshua Tree National Monument on a Sabbath afternoon. Once they arrived at the park, the young pathfinders began to beg, "Please let us climb the rocks!" Next to the parking lot was a hillside of large boulders, which were the perfect challenge for young legs to conquer.

"Yes, of course you may. Just be careful and come right back when you're called for dinner." With those instructions, the happy group of more than thirty young people began scrambling up the rocks around 3:30 in the afternoon.

It was a time to regroup for the tired adults who now had to fix supper for what they knew would be ravenous youngsters when they returned.

Time passed quickly, and at 5:30, one of the adults called on the bull horn "Time for supper! Come on down!"

No response.

Another hour came and went and still no response. Now the anxious adults began to pray and to drive around the area to locate their missing group. As the sun began to set, car lights were turned on, and call after call on the bull horn were made. Earnest prayers were ascending for the lost Pathfinders.

Another hour and another hour passed, but at 8:45 p.m., Jan, one of the junior counselors, arrived at the campsite. She had injured her arm while climbing. She pointed in the direction where the Pathfinders were, so two of the male adults began the ascent over the rocks and up the mountain. It was now very dark, and they were totally dependent on the flashlights they carried. Soon they came to a large chasm. Flashing their lights downward, they estimated there was a fifty-foot drop to the bottom. With a leap, the men jumped the chasm and moved on.

Soon they could hear the voices of the Pathfinders, and after calling and climbing, the men finally located them. But now, the bigger question was, "How do we get these kids off the mountain?" The leaders knew they could not have young Pathfinders jump the fifty-foot chasm, and they were in a quandary in knowing what to do since they were not familiar with this mountain and didn't have any idea how to find a safe way down.

"What shall we do?"

"The best thing we can do is to pray. Let's pray."

And so, there in the middle of the night, over thirty young people bowed their heads asking God for help in their time of need. "Please dear God. We don't know how to get off this mountain. Please show us the way." Immediately, two men approached the group.

"It looks like you need help."

"Oh, yes. We have no idea how to safely get off this mountain."

"Follow us. We'll get you down."

And so, slowly, step-by-step with flashlights glowing, the two strangers guided the Pathfinder group down the mountain.

About thirty minutes later, they reached the campground and as the grateful party turned to thank their benefactors, the two men disappeared. Over thirty people, using their flashlights, looked for their guides and could not find them. Their guides had simply vanished!

Now, they were safely off the mountain with no injuries apart from the female counselor who had injured her arm. Everyone knew God had sent two angels to guide them safely off the mountain in the middle of the night. It was a benchmark experience they would never forget!

*****

While most of us may not recall actually seeing an angel, some have been aware of an angelic presence through other kinds of experiences. Carol knows she did not imagine what she felt, and it confirmed, in her mind, the value of prayer before making an important decision. The committee she was a member of made a choice led by God's Spirit.

*****

There was much excitement in the air! The small Oregon church had been without a pastor for almost a year, and now they had been informed that a pastor and his wife were willing to be interviewed for the job. Carol had been selected, along with several other church members, to be on the search committee for a new pastor, and she, along with the others, was now beginning to collect her thoughts, write down questions, and analyze exactly the type of pastor who could fill the needs of their country church.

Soon the pastor and his wife arrived for an introduction. Since it was a two-church district, selected members from both churches sat at a half-round table to begin posing questions for this dignified man and his wife. An opening prayer, sincerely asking for the guidance of the Holy Spirit, was offered and the meeting began.

As the evening progressed, Carol thought, *This man is a true intellectual. He would be great as a seminary professor. We are a blue-collar community, and while our people are intelligent, he may speak above us. I don't think this is quite the match for our church that I'm looking for.*

Having made up her mind, Carol waited for the secret ballot vote to be taken. Soon, pencils and papers were handed out, and the committee members were told to write "yes" if this man and his wife would be appropriate for the two churches or "no" if they would not be. With those simple instructions, each one picked up their pencils to write. As her pencil touched the paper, Carol was determined to write "no." Suddenly, however, an invisible hand strongly covered her writing hand, and, against her will, Carol wrote "yes." The majority of the committee members voted "yes," and the pastor and his wife were welcomed to be the leaders of the two country churches.

Amazed at what had just happened, Carol did not tell anyone about this experience for fear they would think she was losing her mind. Eventually, she began telling a few others the story of how her angel had directed her hand in writing exactly opposite what she intended to write. It was a benchmark experience; one she would never forget, for she remembers it as if it happened yesterday.

But should anyone truly be surprised? After all, in a sincere prayer that evening, didn't they ask for the Holy Spirit to make the final decision about this pastor? Well, He certainly did!

CHAPTER 22

TRAVELING ON AIR

Some of the people who generously took the time to be interviewed for this book had more than one providential story to share with me. Such was the case of Holly, a twenty-four-year-old maternity nurse who had been a Christian all her life. Her family had consistently made it a practice to have family worship in their home, and Holly had been taught to pray at any early age. Here is her first miracle story, which occurred in 2008:

*****

"Okay, my young friend. Let's head back home. I think I have everything we came for." Margie smiled at eleven-year-old Holly. Margie was happy Holly was able to travel with her on the long trip to Prince George, and Holly's happy conversation had prevented it from being a lonely trip. Margie, a newlywed, was anxious to get back to her wonderful husband, so they began the journey back to her new home.

Traveling on Air

After traveling awhile, Margie glanced down at the gas gauge. "Oh, no!" Her voice had a note of alarm. "I forgot to buy gas! I should have remembered to buy gas after our long trip north!" At once, she began to mentally chastise herself. *How could I have been so forgetful? Here I am responsible for Holly's safety, and we need gas to get home.*

Wondering if she had enough gas to get back to Prince George, she weighed whether she should turn around. Then Holly spoke up. "I saw several gas stations on our trip north. Maybe we can get gas as we go south," she said. Margie relaxed.

"Of course," she agreed, "we'll just pray we have enough gas to get to the next gas station."

With the gauge at E, meaning empty, Margie suggested that they pray. She knew they were two ladies traveling on a highway that had a dangerous reputation. If fact, it was frequently called, "The Highway of Tears." Many abductions and murders had occurred on this very road in the past, and she realized the danger they were in if the car stalled.

"Let's sing and pray!" Margie's voice sounded braver than she felt. "Dear God, here we are, two ladies on a dangerous road with our gas tank at empty. Please keep this car moving. You know we need Your help. Thank you for answering our prayer!" Then they sang and prayed again.

Soon they came to a service station, but a large sign posted said, CLOSED. With a sinking heart, Margie concluded, "We simply need to keep going because now we don't have enough gas to return to Prince George." Now the praying intensified and, to keep their courage up, they sang Christian hymns.

Eventually, another service station appeared, but, again, the sign said CLOSED. Margie realized they were in a truly desperate situation. However, the car kept running. Gas station after gas station was closed, but the car kept running. Finally, an hour and a half after the gas gauge had registered empty, they found a service station that had lights on and was open. With a sigh of relief, they pulled into the first pump and, yes, it's true, the car stalled and came to a complete stop without the brakes being applied. It had no more power!

It was now late at night, but Margie and Holly were not concerned. With a full gas tank and very grateful hearts, they thanked God for His miraculous help in their time of need. What a wonderful story they had to tell their family and friends when they arrived home!

Whether our Father in heaven commanded angels to push their car or to make it run on air, Margie and Holly never knew. They only knew that God truly answered their prayer for safety as they traveled home that dark night. It was a never-to-be-forgotten experience.

CHAPTER 23

STRANGER IN THE NIGHT

> *Isn't it encouraging to know we can call for heaven's help even on a lonely road?*

As I interviewed people and listened to their stories, I was intrigued that several of my friends remembered experiences that involved car trouble. Each situation so impressed them that they remembered it years later and attribute their experience to intervention from heaven because of the physical appearance of their helper and the sudden disappearance of their benefactor. Isn't it encouraging to know we can call for heaven's help even on a lonely road?

*****

The date was around 1982. The time was 11:30 at night. The place was Portland Adventist Medical Center. Darla, a young nurse at the hospital, had just finished working the swing shift, and she noticed how very cold the weather had turned. As she drove home, she realized there was snow and ice on the road. It was really slushy! Heading north on Interstate 205 towards Vancouver, Washington, Darla's tiny Honda Accord soon came behind a large semi-truck. The wheels of the semi kept throwing slush on her windshield, so Darla made the decision to pass the truck. Knowing her small tires needed more speed to pass the truck, Darla hit the gas pedal and then pulled in front of the semi.

It was then that everything went into slow motion. Her car began to spin in front of the semi. "Oh, Lord, this is it!" Darla knew, instantly, that she was going to die. The following few seconds were a blur. The next thing Darla knew her car was sitting in the median strip. *How did I get here?* Darla wondered. Finally, after taking a few deep breaths, Darla opened the car door and stepped outside. The left tire of the car was buried in dirt up to the bumper. What could she do now? It was now around 12:30 a.m., and here she was, a young woman alone, stuck in the mud in the middle of the night!

Getting back into the car and realizing her desperate need, Darla cried out to the Lord. "Lord, please help me. I need help. I can't get out of here!" While she was sitting there, a two-ton, white pickup truck pulled up behind her car. Out stepped a tall (at least 6'3") man in a white, ten-gallon Texas cowboy hat and cowboy boots.

At this point, it's important to digress for a moment to explain what this meant to Darla. You see, Darla had moved from Chicago to the west, and she had a prejudice towards cowboy hats and cowboy boots. Was it due to fear or was it those stories of the wild west she had heard? The very tall man in a very tall cowboy hat sent her mind racing, wondering what situation she had gotten herself into.

"Do you need help?"

"Yes, I'm stuck in the mud."

"No problem. I can get you out," he replied with an assuring voice.

Soon he had a chain hooked on the tiny Honda, pulled it out of the mud, and then moved in front of Darla's car.

"I want to pay you," Darla voice was insistent.

"No, no payment is necessary. Just help someone else who is in need and that will be payment enough," he called back.

"Thank you. Thank you so much!" Now her voice had a special ring to it. Then, looking for her keys, she took her eyes off the white truck. Suddenly, Darla realized the truck had disappeared. Looking up and down the highway in both directions, she felt a strange awe creep over her as she realized what had happened. She had prayed. An answer came soon after her prayer. Her problem had been solved. The man in the ten-gallon hat and white truck had completely vanished. It was miraculous. With a grateful heart, Darla pulled onto the highway towards home.

"Thank you, Lord. Thank you for sending an angel to help me in my predicament!"

*****

Sometimes angels appear to hinder our plans. At least, Holly was irritated because she wasn't getting home quickly. How many times have apparent delays prevented accidents in our own lives? If we could see the big picture, we might be surprised at the many interventions by heavenly agents.

*****

The newborn baby's lusty cry made Holly take a deep breath of relief. At last! It had been an all-night process to bring this little human into the world. As a young midwife-in-training, Holly and her fellow classmates were required to stay with each expectant mother until her baby was born, so Holly had not had rest for about twenty-four hours and was absolutely exhausted.

Clean-up after the delivery took some time, but Holly finally gathered her coat and purse and headed out the hospital door. It was the first snow that winter, and, tired as she was, she didn't think much about icy roads. However, her relationship with the Lord caused her to pray a short prayer. "Dear God, I'm so, so tired. Please help me to get home safely this morning."

As Holly sped on the road towards home, she clipped along at the posted speed limit, not thinking of slowing down for ice. A thought came through her head. Her mother had once said, "Most accidents happen within a mile from people's home." She was now about a mile from home, and looking up, she saw a car preparing to enter the roadway. Suddenly, a red Nissan with flashing lights passed her and positioned itself between her and the other car. Then, the Nissan slowed down to about twenty miles per hour.

What a bother! Holly thought. *What's with this guy? I wish he'd get out of the way, so I can get home!* However, the red Nissan kept its slow, steady pace around a high curve and then on the last straight stretch towards Holly's home.

Suddenly, Holly realized she could not see the Nissan anymore. "Where did he go?" Her eyes scanned the straight stretch. The red car could not have disappeared down any side roads because there were no side roads. It was a puzzle.

When she arrived home, Holly noticed her roommate's car had ice on the windshield, so she decided to scrape that off for her. Susan, her roommate, would be leaving for class soon, so it would save Susan a little time.

The two women greeted each other as Susan hurried out the door and Holly entered. In a few minutes, Holly's cell phone began to buzz. It was a text from Susan. "I had to slow down to about twenty miles an hour on the road this morning. It's very icy. If you go anywhere later today, be sure to drive slowly."

Suddenly, Holly began to be aware of what had happened in the hour before. Being too tired, she had disregarded the icy roads and had traveled full speed to get home for some sleep. The red car with flashing lights had passed her and then slowed down to about twenty miles an hour. It had led her around a curve with no guard rails and a steep drop-off, had led her almost to her home, and it had then disappeared. It was all like a dream, but Holly knew it was so real. "Thank you, Lord, for answering my prayer when I started home. Thank you for sending my guardian angel to lead me home safely."

Later, Holly told her family, "I think my guardian angel drives a red Nissan." And Holly was so grateful the Lord orchestrated a scenario, which she saw with her own eyes, and in which she could sense His love and care for her. He had faithfully answered her prayer for safety.

*****

Have you ever had an experience when you cannot explain the outcome except to credit heaven for the result? Marianne has such a story, and even though her encounter happened many years ago, she is still very convinced it was angels who drove her car early one morning.

*****

As a nurse, Marianne was required to be at work by 6:45 a.m. That meant she must leave her home by 6:00 in the morning. She had safely done this for years without mishap; however, this November morning was dark and very foggy, so visibility was unusually poor. Wanting to get to work on time, Marianne traveled down Lake Creek Road when immediately in front of the car, she saw the neighbor's cow lying on the road. Swerving to miss it, she soon saw other cows' large bodies seeking the warmth of the concrete road. "I don't know how I drove through them without hitting a cow. I believe an angel helped me make it through that herd of cows lying in the road." This experience made a deep impression on Marianne's mind and convinced her of God's protective care.

Perhaps we can credit Marianne's experience with the biblical promise found in Psalms 91:11, 12: "For he shall give his angels charge over thee, to keep thee in all thy ways. They shall bear thee up in their hands, lest thou dash thy foot against a stone." It will be so interesting to listen to the stories our guardian angels will relate to us in heaven. Marianne's angel will probably begin, "And do you remember that November morning when you were going to work? It took fast action to keep you from hitting those cows. Here's what happened...."

> *Do you remember that November morning? It took fast action to keep you from hitting those cows.*

CHAPTER 24

SOMETIMES PRETTY, SOMETIMES NOT

When heavenly angels appear so they can be visible to human eyes, are they always beautiful? Many people describe them as good-looking and well-dressed. Dawn would agree. Some describe angels appearing as the very elderly. Whatever form in which they appear, they are always helpful.

*****

Dawn and her mother were driving a small Datsun across eastern Oregon. The land was desert-like and quite desolate. Suddenly, their tiny car began to sputter and spit, and they realized they were two women in an isolated area with a car that had broken down and without the ability to fix it. So… they prayed. Eventually, an old farmer came by, lifted the hood, and after analyzing the situation, said, "I don't think I can help you."

After he left a large diesel truck with a trailer stopped. The driver's countenance caught Dawn's attention. It was more than handsome. It was beautiful with the kindest expression imaginable. Dawn's father was a truck driver, so she had some idea of the kind of work the truck driver must do to maintain his vehicle. And that work resulted in rough, hard-working hands. However, when this truck driver with the beautiful face took off the gloves he was wearing, he did not have rough truck driver's hands. They were beautiful to look at.

After checking out the small Datsun, he also said, "I can't fix this. I'll give you a ride to the nearest Datsun agency." Dawn and her mother climbed into the truck and soon arrived at the Datsun office. Before they could thank the kind truck driver or even say goodbye, he had left. Dawn often wondered if that man with the beautiful, kindest face and the beautiful hands was an angel sent to meet their need while stranded on an isolated road.

Psalms 34:7 tells us, "The angel of the LORD encampeth round about them that fear him, and delivereth them." Many of God's people have found this promise to be absolutely true! Praise His holy name!

*****

Dawn has another story to share. Living in a part of the country where the weather can change quickly, she found herself in a dangerous situation. Her story has a familiar ring to it. See what you think.

*****

"Dawn, my plane leaves at 3:00 tomorrow afternoon. Can you take me and Mark to the airport?"

Dawn looked at her schedule to see what she could do and decided she could make the seventy-five-mile trip. The next day, the trip through the countryside was uneventful, and Dawn enjoyed the scenery as they passed the farmhouses with many acres surrounding them.

Once they arrived at the airport and goodbyes were said, Dawn began the long trip home. Suddenly and unexpectedly, a snowstorm that quickly turned into a blizzard began to obscure the road. For about half an hour, Dawn fought to see through the windshield and could not even see the middle of the road. Realizing that at any moment she could land in a ditch and would not be seen until the storm cleared, Dawn began to pray. "Father, please help me!"

Dawn describes what happened next. "After I prayed, immediately a dark SUV came behind me as if it had dropped from the sky. Then he passed me and drove slowly enough, so I could follow his tracks in the snow. He led me for five to ten minutes until the storm cleared. Then he disappeared suddenly." After that, Dawn could see the road and was able to get home.

Was this just happenstance? How was the SUV driver able to see Dawn's car without colliding with her? How did he feel safe in passing her in a blizzard? How was her prayer answered immediately? How did the SUV disappear immediately after leading her through the blizzard? Perhaps heaven will have answers for all of those questions. Until then, we are so grateful for our Father in heaven's help when His children call to Him.

*****

We all know angels are super strong. However, when their strength is displayed, it always produces a sense of awe in us. Even Tiffany's children knew the strong man was not an ordinary man.

*****

Tiffany Bridges often liked to drive around with her two young children in the van just to get out of the house and to add some diversion to their lives. So, when her housework was done, Tiffany called to her boys. "Okay, guys, let's go. There's a country road we haven't explored yet, so if all your jobs are done, we'll go see where that road leads."

Soon, two young boys and their mother were strapped under seat belts to begin another adventure. Finding the country road, Tiffany turned and noticed that this was indeed different than where their usual escapades led them, for there were no houses along the way. Only miles and miles of trees.

After realizing that this road didn't offer much excitement for her boys, Tiffany decided to turn around. Making the turn on the narrow road was challenging, and suddenly, one of the back wheels fell into a ditch on the side of the road.

Trying again and again to drive the car onto the road left Tiffany in frustration, and fear began to creep into her mind. She had forgotten her cellphone at home. They were on a very lonely road, and there were no houses nearby where she could get help. What to do?

"Mom, let's pray." Her boys could easily see the predicament they were in. And so, they prayed. "Dear God, here we are stuck in a ditch, and no one is near to help us. Please send help."

Tiffany explains what happened next.

Suddenly, out of nowhere, a man appeared beside my window. I rolled the window down a little bit. He asked, "Do you need help?"

"Yes," I replied, "My back tire is in the ditch."

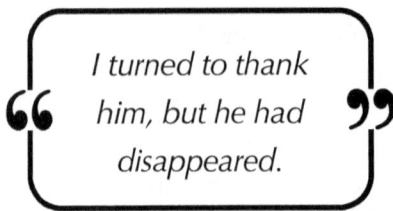

> I turned to thank him, but he had disappeared.

After he went to the back of the van, we could feel the van being lifted as he literally picked it up to set it back on the road. I turned to thank him, but he had disappeared. None of us could see where he went. There was no place for him to go except, perhaps, behind a tree. My children felt that God had sent an angel to our rescue. Whether or not he was an angel, we know for sure that our prayer was answered on that lonely country road.

*****

Mary told me a story that happened years ago. Again, her car seemed to have no weight at all. Or does weight really matter in heavenly hands?

*****

Mary closed the door to the hospital slowly as she stepped onto the parking lot and into the icy wind. More than one thought caused Mary to be cautious. It was past midnight, and she well knew the danger of a young woman alone in that part of the city. With a quick survey of the parking lot, she made her way across the icy pavement to her car. Once safely in her car, Mary had time to assess what was going on in her life.

Here she was, a young nurse, working the 4:00 p.m. to 12:00 a.m. shift in the emergency room at the Washington Sanitarium in Washington, D.C. Her soldier husband, Bob, was working in Operation White Coat for the U.S. Army, but that night, he lay very sick in the Walter Reed Medical Center. Mary and baby Leslie, along with Mary's mother, had moved from sunny California to the east to be closer to Bob during his army tenure at Fort Dietrich, Maryland. Now Bob was so sick, a friend told Mary, that he might be dying.

It all seemed so overwhelming. It was the middle of the night; Bob was sick in the hospital,; they had a newborn baby; and freezing weather made driving home hazardous. Life was stressful.

We'll let Mary tell the rest of the story in her own words:

As I drove closer to the old apartment building we were living in, I quickly scanned both sides of the street, looking for a parking space. We were required to follow strict parking rules there. We could not use a driveway to park in, and as far as I could see, there was only one more parking spot left on an incline. I pulled up beside the car in front of the empty space and slowly tried to parallel park. The car wheels could not gain traction on the ice, and, try as I might, I could not ease the car into the space. The nose of the car was still in the street, and I was afraid the police would tow it away if I left it there. Also, if I double-parked, my car was certain to be impounded.

Over and over, I tried to park the car but with no success. Finally, I got out of the car to find something to put under the wheel to get traction. I found an old plastic tablecloth and put it under the tire, but the car kept slipping. I knew I was in a serious situation in the middle of the night. In desperation I put my head on the steering wheel and prayed, "Lord, what shall I do now?"

Suddenly, I heard a tap on the car window. There stood a nice-looking young man in a white suit. (How many men do you see in white suits with snow on the ground in the middle of the night?) Not sure what to think, I carefully rolled down the window a little bit. He said, "If you do exactly what I tell you to do, the car will go into the parking space. Keep your foot on the brake and place your other foot on the accelerator." As I followed his direction, he simply pushed the car into the parking space as easily as if it were a feather. I looked down at my feet and thought, *Wow!* Glancing up, I tried to find the helpful young man to thank him, but he was nowhere to be seen.

I locked the car and entered the apartment building. As I came in the front door, my mother stared at me.

"What happened to you?" Her voice had a sense of awe.

"What do you mean? I've just gotten off of work and have tried to park the car. A young man in a white suit helped me park the car. It was miraculous."

"Well," Mom explained, "When you came in the door, there was a light surrounding you."

Mom and I concluded that it was definitely my guardian angel who helped me that night.

CHAPTER 25

ANGEL VOICES

Ten-year-old Moriah and her brother, Benny, lived with their parents on a ten-acre parcel of land in southern Minnesota. It was their custom to have morning and evening worship with scripture reading, songs, and prayer, asking for God's guidance and protection for each day. During the spring and summer months, the grass grew quickly in that area, and it became a hiding place for snakes and other vermin. To keep everyone safe, the family decided to work together to keep the grass mowed down. Dad Brown would mow the large, lower portion of their land with a rider mower, and Mother Brown and the two children could help him by mowing the smaller, upper portion with the gas mower.

One day, Benny began his part of the commitment by mowing the upper part of their property. Because it was a hot, tiring job, Mother Brown carefully kept track of how long each of her children mowed, so they felt it was fair, and they could take turns without becoming exhausted.

When Benny's turn was up, Moriah took hold of the mower's handle and concentrated on the tall grass in front of her. Suddenly, she heard her mother's call. Being an obedient young girl, she left the mower running (the old lawn mowers did not have a handle release shut-off) and hurried to the house. Mother saw her coming and wondered why Moriah was running to the house. She was supposed to be mowing the lawn.

All of a sudden, a huge explosion rang through the air. The gas lawn mower had exploded sending shrapnel in every direction. Fortunately, Moriah was out of harm's way as the metal pieces flew everywhere. When she arrived at the house, mother asked Moriah, "Why did you come?"

"Well, I heard you calling me. That's why I ran to the house," Moriah explained.

Mother was amazed. "But I didn't call you, Moriah. It must have been your guardian angel's voice you heard calling your name."

Worship that evening had sincere prayers of thanks for Moriah's protection from certain death. Her angel called before the lawn mower exploded and brought Moriah a safe distance from the sharp metal pieces. Praise God for guardian angels! And praise God Moriah had been taught prompt obedience to respond when she heard her name called.

*****

Angels generally remain hidden from our eyesight, but, occasionally, they reveal themselves in human form. In this next story, Barry did not see an angel, but he definitely heard one. He had no doubt that one of these heavenly beings spoke to him, and he would agree with the following quotation:

> *Barry did not see an angel, but he definitely heard one.*

"Are they not all ministering spirits, sent forth to minister for them who shall be heirs of salvation?" These messages are coming down the line to our time, to them that shall be heirs of salvation. Angels actually come to our world. Nor are they always invisible. They sometimes veil their angelic appearance, and appearing as men, they converse with and enlighten human beings. (*My Life Today*, p. 304)

Read Barry's incredible story and mark how God led a man from the depths of sin to a transformed life.

*****

Barry sat in his comfortable chair one Friday evening, bored with life, so he turned on the TV. As he waited for a program to come on the screen, he remembered how life had taken him on a twisted road ever since early childhood. His grandmother and an aunt were pious women who taught young Barry many precious Bible truths. But, later in boarding school, a principal insisted that Barry give information about one of his classmates. Incensed, Barry left the school, determined never to look back. The following years were filled with success in business, learning to be a professional hypnotist, two marriages, enjoying being father to one daughter, and putting behind the truths he had learned. Yes, the past forty years had been challenging, but some goals had been reached.

I'll change stations, Barry thought. He started to push the button on the remote control, but a loud commanding voice said, "STOP!" Startled, Barry looked around. Since he now lived alone, he wondered if someone had entered his home. He knew he wasn't drunk, since he didn't drink, and he wasn't using drugs. After convincing himself that he was alone in the house, Barry now turned his attention to the program on the air. What was this KBLN and 3ABN? He hadn't ever heard of them.

As he watched program after program, tears began to flow as he recognized the biblical truths he had learned as a young man. He now realized that the Voice he had heard was not that of a human but was the Lord speaking to him. In the early morning hours, an evangelist made an appeal for his audience to make a full surrender to Christ. Barry fell to his knees asking God for forgiveness, realizing the presence of the Holy Spirit was very real in the room, as he sobbed his repentance for the many years serving the Lord's enemy.

Subsequently, Barry began his journey back to the Lord. With God's help, he made many changes in his life. Miracle after miracle occurred in his life as he prayed for deliverance from his smoking habit, drinking twelve cups of coffee every day, wrong reading habits, eating unclean foods, off-color jokes, immoral sites on the computer. Day by day, his life was cleaned up, and Barry became a new man in Christ.

Eventually, Barry was ordained as an elder in the church, and he became an active support and participant in his local congregation. Friends who had prayed for him for forty years were thrilled, and Barry's new life was a genuine blessing to all those who associated with him.

Barry is now resting in Jesus and awaiting the resurrection. None of us who heard his story will forget how he was always brought to tears as he told it. Realizing that he had resisted the Holy Sprit's impressions many times in the past, he wondered if the voice which so loudly commanded "STOP" was the last call to repentance. How grateful Barry was that he obeyed that call!

Yes, miracles do happen even today. A 180-degree turn in a genuine conversion is not humanmade. Only God can change a heart and make it new!

*****

Sometimes, angels simply pick us up. At least, that is what Brock thinks is what must have happened. He has no other explanation for his fast action.

*****

The sudden explosion, caused by ice water contacting hot glass, sent glass flying through the air. All of this happened just minutes after young Brock Smith and his family had started on their vacation and were looking for good times ahead. As they traveled through Sacramento in their station wagon, Brock's dad asked, "Brock, could you climb in the back and put those soda pop bottles in the ice chest? There's just ice water in the chest now, but it should cool down the soda pop."

"Sure, Dad, I'll do that." And with a quick turn, Brock flipped over the back seat of the car to the end of the station wagon where his two sisters were playing (this was the day before seat belts were required or cars had air conditioners).

"Whew, it must be about 115 degrees in here!" Dad's voice sounded concerned as he rolled down the window.

"Excuse me, girls," Brock said. "Dad wants me to put those pop bottles in the ice chest." Brock positioned himself between his sisters on the right side and the ice chest on the left. He picked up the hot soda pop bottles and threw them in the ice water in the chest.

Suddenly, the next thing Brock knew, he was bowed over in front of his sisters with his left arm over his eyes. The hot glass contacting the ice-cold water sent glass flying through the air and left a gash in Brock's left arm.

"Dad, my arm's bleeding a lot!" Brock's voice shook with fear.

His mother, a nurse, immediately panicked, but his dad kept his cool and instructed, "Take your t-shirt off and wrap it around your arm. That should stop the bleeding."

Then dad hit the gas pedal, hoping the police would stop him and then guide him to the hospital. It turned out that they found the hospital themselves, and by the time they reached it, the bleeding in Brock's arm had stopped. His wound only required three stitches, and now, after all the excitement, their family could continue the long planned-for vacation.

Looking back on that experience, Brock wonders how, even if he had anticipated the explosion of the bottles, he could have moved so rapidly to protect his sisters and to cover his eyes. He realized that he could not have done all of that even with the advantage of foresight. It all happened with such speed that he is convinced he had heavenly help to land where he did, as quickly as he did, and, as a result, greater tragedy didn't occur. Praise God for His protection as we pray for safety! Our angels must move with swift action so many times in our lives to keep us from harm and danger.

CHAPTER 26

THE PRECISE INVASION

One of the most amazing rescues in America history happened in Los Baños in the Philippines. My husband has a friend, Sarah, who he has known since they were in the third grade together. Sarah lived through this experience. "You ought to get Sarah's story," he would tell me. "It's incredible!"

And incredible it is. Sarah, who is now in her eighties, distinctly remembers the drama that surrounded her on that amazing day in 1945. I think you will agree that many prayers were answered then, and angels must have been very busy protecting the prisoners, so the human plans could move along flawlessly.

*****

The Japanese flat-bed truck came to a skidding stop as dust flew in every direction. Instantly, Japanese soldiers jumped down and ran to the door of the house, banging on it until it flew open. "*Torakko no ushiro ni noro!*" ("Get on the back of the truck!") they screamed, motioning towards the door and the truck and waving their guns in a threatening manner towards the family inside.

The American missionary family had expected the soldiers to arrive since hearing of Japan's invasion of the Philippines. Dr. Philip and Dr. Marianne took the hands of three-year-old Sarah and six-year-old Billy, while also grabbing suitcases filled with items that they anticipated they would need in a prison camp. Obediently, they filed out towards the truck and found other Americans were already seated there with a look of shock on their faces.

Japan had invaded the Philippines in that year, 1942, and all Americans, Europeans, Australians, and Canadians on the island were being transported to Los Baños, a sixty acre prison camp on the island. The camp barracks were being built out of bamboo by 800 men who first arrived as prisoners. Seven hundred additional prisoners arrived by 1944. The bamboo barracks, with no hint of privacy, were to be the home of more than 2,000 prisoners for the next few years.

Sarah's parents, both graduates from the Loma Linda College of Medical Evangelists, had come to the Philippines as missionaries a short time before. The days since their arrival in the Philippines had been full of drama, as they ran to raid shelters to avoid the Japanese bombs. Now, their lives had taken a tragic turn, as they were housed in barracks with only a pot in the room for a latrine and rice with worms were their daily fare. Sarah's mother, when relating their experience later said, "First, the prisoners removed the worms, then they removed the rice, then they just ate the worms and the rice." And as the days rolled by, less and less rice was served. Dr. Marianne developed beriberi, and other prisoners began to die from malnutrition and other diseases.

In spite of the primitive, grim lifestyle Sarah and her family were subjected to, the children in the camp still found ways to entertain themselves. The game "Mother May I?" was a favorite of the youngsters, and Sarah remembers playing with the other children in the middle of the camp. The Japanese soldiers were not in that part of the camp, and the children were allowed to play and even exchange Christmas gifts during the holiday season. Since no one had money and stores were not available, they all traded toys, and Sarah remembers receiving a doll with papier mâché arms, legs, and broken head, which they tried to patch. Her brother, Billy, received marbles and a toy canoe. The prisoners were also allowed to have church services on the Sabbath, and Sarah recalls the bench she sat on, while they sang and listened to one of the prisoners preach.

Three years went by, and the prisoners were anxious to know what was happening in the world. When would they be set free? Of course, radios or any other form of communication were not allowed and would mean instant execution if the enemy suspected a prisoner to have one. But that did not stop the intense desire of those in the camp to know what was going on in the outside world. Eventually, a radio had been smuggled into the camp and was disassembled. Its parts were given to various prisoners, and no one knew who had what part. Then, at an appointed time, they would come together, assemble the radio, and listen in secret. This was how the prisoners learned that General McArthur was planning an invasion of the Philippines. What excitement! How many prayers must have gone up for a successful invasion!

Meanwhile, Philippine guerillas closely watched the camp from the surrounding jungle, noting that the Japanese soldiers did their daily calisthenics at 7:00 in the morning. The Japanese guns were stockpiled in a teepee fashion away from the exercise area. The guerillas transmitted this valuable information to the American forces.

The prisoners knew that tension was building when they were told to dig trenches. They realized the trenches were to be their own graves after their execution. Later, they learned that all 2,147 prisoners were to be executed on February 23, 1945.

However, our Father in heaven had a different plan for those prisoners, and it was to be carried out in four phases:

Phase I – The 11th Airborne's Provisional Reconnaissance Platoon guided by twenty Filipino guerrillas would use local fishing boats to travel across Laguna Lake on February 21. They would arrive at Los Baños by 7:00 a.m. on February 23.

Phase II – Company B, 1st Battalion, 511th PIR would fly low and jump to a zone near the camp and release the prisoners at 7:00 a.m. on February 23.

Phase III – The 672nd Amphibian Tractor Battalion would send fifty-four amphibious vehicles across Laguna Bay to rendezvous about two miles from Los Baños. They would arrive at Los Baños at 7:00 a.m.

Phase IV – Company C of the 637th Tank Destroyer Battalion and the 188th Glider Infantry Regiment joined together to fight enemy resistance, if necessary (Sovereign Media and Homestead Communications, www.warfarehistorynetwork.com, [accessed April 5, 2024]).

That February 23 morning was a Sabbath. Suddenly, at 7:00 a.m., the prisoners at Los Baños heard the sound of many planes flying very low overhead. Paratroopers of the 511th Parachute Infantry Regiment began jumping from the planes at 500 feet (barely enough height for their chutes to open), and a grenade was thrown on the Japanese rifles, completely disarming the Japanese soldiers. This, of course, left many of the Japanese soldiers without any defense, but some escaped into the jungle.

By sea and by land, the American and Filipino guerilla forces were timed to arrive at the same time as the paratroopers. Fifty-four amphibious tractors (Amtracs) arrived in nine lines with six per line. The prisoners were very quickly told to move out of the camp. Sarah remembers the confusion that existed as the American soldiers began directing the prisoners towards the camp gate. Some of the prisoners refused to leave (probably due to shock and confused thinking due to malnutrition). In order to encourage all to leave the camp, American soldiers set fire to the bamboo barracks.

Because Sarah's mother was so ill, she was put on one of the first Amtracs to leave the camp. All the women and children were put on Amtracs, and the men well enough to walk followed behind. They were taken across Laguna Bay where ambulances were waiting on the other side for the very ill. Sarah recalls looking at the American soldiers and thinking how big and how healthy they looked!

The facility they were now in also had a hospital tent next to it. The children would go in to talk with the wounded soldiers, and one soldier gave Sarah the first chocolate she had ever eaten. The soldiers also gave the children a ride on a truck. After one of these excursions, Sarah forgot her shoes on the truck, but a soldier retrieved the shoes and returned them to her. And what pathetic shoes they were! So worn out that they had to be tied on Sarah's feet.

The prisoners were kept at this camp for several weeks, slowly regaining their strength with carefully prepared food. Finally, the day came when they could board an ocean liner and head towards home. Sarah remembers going under the Golden Gate Bridge and seeing her aunt and grandpa waiting for them. They had not seen each other for six years.

And so, once again, our Father in heaven enabled several forces to come together to rescue His children. Many prayers were answered that

Sabbath morning as by air, by land, and by sea, 2,147 prisoners of war were safely transported to freedom and able to begin a normal life once again. A flawless rescue that, even now at age 83, Sarah remembers as completely miraculous.

*****

I decided to include this last story because it happened to my father while I was an infant. It is just one of the many examples of God's intervention for our family, which I find to be encouraging, and it provides hope for the future as this world ricochets towards its end. Where God placed us at the end of the story was exactly where we needed to be to meet a dedicated Bible worker, who explained many truths to my parents. How grateful I am for His leading!

*****

My father was stationed in Hawaii as a radioman for the U.S. Navy during World War II. Probably because of the beauty of the islands and because he was missing us, Dad decided to prepare a Quonset hut on the beach, so Mom and I could join him. However, he was notified that he and several other men were to be honorably discharged in the final phases of the war. This came about very quickly and unexpectedly.

Meanwhile, Mom and I were in a motel in San Francisco waiting to board a ship to the islands. She sent a trunk ahead loaded with items that were valuable to them, assuming Dad would pick it up at the dock. When Dad learned he would be coming back to the mainland, he knew he had to inform my mother of the change of plans, but there was one problem. He knew we were somewhere in San Francisco, but he had no idea which motel we were staying in. Another complicating factor was that the trans-Pacific telephone cable did not transmit messages very clearly. Would Mom be able to understand what he was attempting to communicate?

Dad prayed. He asked the Lord to help him locate Mom in that vast city, so she and I would not be traveling west to the islands while he was traveling east. Then he picked up the phone and dialed the operator. He explained that he had no idea which motel his wife and his child were staying in, but asked if she would be willing to begin calling the motels in San Francisco. It must have sounded like a wild and unreasonable request to that operator, but it was wartime, and she understood Dad's dilemma and determined to help him.

The operator picked a motel, dialed the number, and asked if my mother was residing there. Wonder of wonders! It was exactly that motel where we were staying. Think of it. Dozens of motels in San Francisco, yet the first the operator dialed was the right motel! Then, with much background interference, Dad was able to transmit the message, "Don't come, don't come." With those sketchy instructions, my mother left San Francisco, and we traveled south to stay with her sister in Escondido.

The Lord wanted us to live in Escondido long enough to meet Mrs. Harcourt, a dedicated Bible worker, who introduced my parents to the book *The Great Controversy*, which changed the course of our lives. Later, both of my parents were baptized into the Seventh-day Adventist Church, and I had the privilege of receiving the benefits of Adventist living and an Adventist education.

My father repeated this story more than once through the years since he was convinced God had answered his prayer to find Mother and me in the vast city of San Francisco. How grateful I am that he had enough spiritual sensitivity and faith to petition heaven in his time of need! And what happened to their trunk of valuables that had been sent west? It was never found. But that trunk of treasures could not compare with the treasures of truth our family learned because of God's leading those many years ago when the telephone operator dialed the right number on her first attempt to find us. What a God we serve!

CHAPTER 27

STEPS TO ANSWERED PRAYER

As we think of the nearly eight billion inhabitants on planet earth and the comparatively few people interviewed for this book, we realize these stories represent only a tip of the iceberg of the celestial activity going on here and now. Millions and millions of similar stories are waiting to be told. Our Father in heaven is as willing today, as in the ancient past, to positively touch the lives of His children who have faith in Him. But are there steps we must follow for answered prayer? Is there a science for answered prayer?

> *Our Father in heaven is as willing today, as in the ancient past, to positively touch the lives of His children who have faith in Him.*

The Latin word *scientia* is defined as "a knowledge." The English word science is derived from this Latin term, so we use the word science when describing how to successfully complete different activities in life. There is a science in good cooking, a science in successfully handling money, a science in raising godly children, etc. Just so, there is a science in reaching the goal of answered prayer. Let's take a look at the science, or the knowledge, we need to reach that goal.

Roger Morneau, a genuine prayer warrior and researcher, has written four books on the topic of prayer: *Trip into the Supernatural, Incredible Answers to Prayer, More Incredible Answers to Prayer,* and *The Incredible Power of Prayer.* Mr. Morneau granted my husband and me a three-hour visit with him and his wife in their Modesto, California, home. On that Saturday night, my husband took notes as this prayer warrior outlined several important steps that are necessary for our requests to be heard in heaven. I will list them numerically:

1. We must put sin out of our lives. Now, this is not an easy task, and we need the Lord's help to complete step number one. A good prayer would be, "Lord, please forgive me for every one of my sins (it is good to be very specific here). I know I have caused sorrow to Your heart so many times. I claim Jesus as my Savior and know You will forgive me. Please show me if there is anything offensive to You in my life. Is there anything I need to give up, anything I need to make right with someone else, anything for which I need to make restitution? Please give me Your power to do this." As, point by point, the Holy Spirit brings to our mind the changes that need to be made and we cooperate with Him, we will be filled with the peace of heaven and are ready to "come boldly unto the throne of grace" (Heb. 4:16). As we realize our right standing with God, our confidence increases for 2 Chronicles 16:9 says, "The eyes of the LORD run to and fro throughout the whole earth, to shew himself strong in the behalf of them whose heart is perfect toward him."

2. We must pray to be filled with the Holy Spirit, so our requests are appropriate and not self-seeking. For instance, if we are praying for the latest Rolls-Royce, it is unlikely our request will be granted. But if we are pleading the unselfish prayer for the salvation of our loved ones, heaven moves into action to begin answering our request. The

Holy Spirit is our safe Leader to guide our thoughts, and we must ask for His presence every day. Our Father in heaven will answer that prayer for Luke 11:13 assures us, "If ye then, being evil, know how to give good gifts unto your children: how much more shall your heavenly Father give the Holy Spirit to them that ask him?"

3. We must always pray for God's will to be done as we make specific requests, and we must have faith that our Father in heaven will answer our prayer according to His perfect will. Matthew 21:22 states, "And all things, whatsoever ye shall ask in prayer, believing, ye shall receive." And, again, we are reassured in John 14:12, 13, "Verily, verily, I say unto you, He that believeth on me, the works that I do he shall do also; and greater works than these shall he do; because I go unto my Father. And whatsoever ye shall ask in my name, that will I do, that the Father may be glorified in the Son."

4. Our prayers must not be languid, sporadic, and carelessly presented. If we truly are wanting our prayers to be answered, we must earnestly, respectfully seek God with our whole heart and be willing to spend significant time as we petition Him. As we open our hearts to Him, He is more than willing to listen and to answer our requests in His own time and in His own way.

5. Matthew 6:9–13 tells us to whom our prayers should be addressed. "Our Father which art in heaven…" (verse 9) is how Jesus explained to His disciples the Person to whom we should direct our prayers. Because Jesus is our heavenly Mediator, who is on the right hand of our Father, we should close our prayers "in Jesus' name, Amen."

6. "The effectual fervent prayer of a righteous man availeth much" (James 5:16), and corporate prayer is even more powerful for Matthew 18:20 states, "For where two or three are gathered together in my name, there am I in the midst of them." Your personal prayer time is so essential to your spiritual well-being. If you can find a prayer partner to consistently pray with, be prepared to see miraculous answers to your prayers.

7. Claim the blood of Jesus for those on your prayer list. Also, ask that the Holy Spirit will work in a powerful way to encourage them to follow the path of righteousness. The Holy Spirit will never force the will of any individual, but He can use many approaches to

encourage one to make the right choice. In fact, He can make it difficult for one to make the wrong choice.

8. Pray for the forgiveness of the sins of those who you are on your prayer list. Be as specific as possible. If these persons are so deceived by Satan, they may not be interested or even able to pray for the forgiveness of their own sins.
9. As you claim the blood of Jesus, ask that the Holy Spirit be present, and pray for the forgiveness of sins those of your prayer list, pray for protection for you, your family, and those who you are specifically praying for. This heavenly protection is very necessary because the devil will react when those under his power are being released. This step is very important!
10. Mr. Morneau explained to us that many times the situation under the devil's control may get worse as the battle between holy and unholy angels intensifies. Then, he said, it is time to pray even more until the power of evil is broken.
11. He also suggested the daily reading of Matthew 27:21–54, which are the final scenes of Christ's life here on earth. We are humbled, made grateful, and drawn closer to our Savior as we review the incredible sacrifice Jesus made for each one of us.
12. If we are truly serious about wanting answers to our prayers, it is important to fast from food, media, or any other distractions so that our minds are clear and the Holy Spirit can communicate what He knows we need to hear.

In closing, I would like to suggest that, after putting the above information in place, you keep a journal of the time and date of your prayers. Then begin recording the answers to your prayers. It will greatly encourage you and others to keep praying. You will experience heaven's answers, which will bring much happiness to you and those you love. May God bless you!

BIBLIOGRAPHY

Morneau, Roger. *Incredible Answers to Prayer.* Hagerstown, MD: Review and Herald Publishing Association, 1990.

Roberts II, Donald J. "The Los Baños Raid: WWII's Finest Allied Mission?" Sovereign Media and Homestead Communications. www.warfarehistorynetwork.com (accessed April 5, 2024).

White, Ellen G. *Child Guidance.* Washington, D.C.: Review and Herald Publishing Association, 1954.

———. *Christ's Object Lessons.* Washington, D.C.: Review and Herald Publishing Association, 1900.

———. *Evangelism.* Washington, D.C.: Review and Herald Publishing Association, 1946.

———. *Gospel Workers.* Battle Creek, MI: Review and Herald Publishing Co., 1892.

———. *Ministry of Healing.* Mountain View, CA: Pacific Press Publishing Association, 1905.

———. *My Life Today.* Washington, D.C.: Review and Herald Publishing Association, 1952.

———. *Steps to Christ.* Mountain View, CA.: Pacific Press Publishing Association, 1892.

———. *Testimonies for the Church*, vol. 1. Mountain View, CA: Pacific Press Publishing Association, 1855.

———. *Testimonies for the Church*, vol. 6. Mountain View, CA: Pacific Press Publishing Association, 1901.

———. *The Adventist Home.* Hagerstown, MD: Review and Herald Publishing Association, 1952.

TEACH Services, Inc.
PUBLISHING

We invite you to view the complete
selection of titles we publish at:
www.TEACHServices.com

We encourage you to write us
with your thoughts about this,
or any other book we publish at:
info@TEACHServices.com

TEACH Services' titles may be purchased in
bulk quantities for educational, fund-raising,
business, or promotional use.
bulksales@TEACHServices.com

Finally, if you are interested in seeing
your own book in print, please contact us at:
publishing@TEACHServices.com

We are happy to review your manuscript at no charge.

www.ingramcontent.com/pod-product-compliance
Lightning Source LLC
Chambersburg PA
CBHW070542170426
43200CB00011B/2516